THE BODY AWAKENS

by Mona Delfino

ISBN: 978-1-6884-5062-2

This book is dedicated to my children:
Leah, Rachel, and Joshua, who have become a light to the world in
their own ways. They are my best friends, and my pride and joy! ~

Contents

PREFACE

"We are slowed down sound and light waves, a walking bundle of frequencies tuned into the cosmos. We are souls dressed up in sacred biochemical garments and our bodies are the instruments through which our souls play their music." - Unknown

I am very happy to bring you a book that I decided to write as a sequel to my first book called *The Sacred Language of the Human Body*. I am a Medical Intuitive/Shaman who has worked independently as a healer for over 40 years. It is truly my passion to help people heal. I have been reading energy since I was a child, and dedicated my whole life to energy, cause and effect, alchemy, sound, light, and to reading and recognizing the deepest part of someone's history. For it's there in the spirit that we have our real freedom. Yet, many feel condensed down into a body that hurts, that is fragile, and we don't know how to change that. Doctors are secondary to the real healing.

Dr. Bruce Lipton mentions that chemical medicine from a doctor works in the body, but only about 2%. Energy work, he says, has anywhere from 97% to 100% effect. Where do these patterns, pains, ideas about living come from? Not only in the way we are raised, but we have past lives. Those lifetimes are what we came in with, and now we are bringing them altogether, (like the pages of a calendar) to heal them in one lifetime!

In the world we live in today, we are being encouraged by the universe with all its astrological effects, to change, mold, merge and create a life of comprehension and understanding in ways that are directly related to **you**. It is my hope and vision that you will receive the intention I have written to help guide you, shed some light on your life, with the knowledge I have been given by experience and as a complete conduit for the Supreme Being. May you recognize, live, and thrive in a way you never imagined, and may this bring you the gifts you have always wanted - and so much more!

CHAPTER ONE
~ THE GROWING MIND ~

These times are challenging, and I don't think anyone would disagree! It's challenging for us on an individual level, and obviously in our world. From day to day, we listen to more things on the news that are frightening and even spooky. We aren't sure of anything anymore. Our days seem shorter and time seems to be speeding up. Certainly, we are recognizing that nothing seems to be the same as it used to be, no matter how we look at life. The newsflash is: "nothing will ever be the same again."

I feel it is extremely important to explain that we are in a time period of expanded awareness. However, to get to a place of comprehension and eventually, acceptance of a deeper awareness, we will have to listen quietly and become still within. We need to stretch ourselves now for our lives to become more peaceful within and without. For example, when in the past we would say no to someone if they requested something from us, today we may think twice and actually do what they request. The attitude of "why not?" may inspire a different take on a new experience!

As for expanding our minds to new perceptions and learning to open our minds, we might remember some of these quotes for starters:

"For it is in the stillness of the mind that the whole universe surrenders." - Rumi

"Once you open your eyes, you can't look back."
- Unknown

"Minds are like parachutes; They only function when open." - Thomas Dewar

The point of that profound quote by Rumi suggests to me that the mind grows with silence.

The growing mind is waking to the essentials of living in today's world. It means a whole new way of recognizing the spirit within coming forth into awareness. We are living in extraordinary times, and old indoctrinated methods of living are found to be outdated. It's like we grew out of our old shoes and are fitting ourselves consciously into new ones for a deeper and clearer foundation; something that gives us room to grow, to walk our talk on a path of empowerment and integrity.

Finally, after 26,000 years, we are becoming remarkable beings with new scientific data that backs up new cell growth, stem cell technology, and recognition of intuition and energy medicine, to name a few. Dr. Masaru Emoto was exceptional in shifting the minds of people and expanding their knowledge to see that water changes at a molecular level when a word that engages feeling is spoken, and the intent toward the water creates a connection to and from the heart. So, whether it takes science to factually encourage new perceptions, or our mind to incorporate more "A-HA" moments in order to comprehend expanded awareness, the good news is that it's happening.

The world sees the proof of this by watching how we are becoming more independent as a society: waking up to GMO's, Monsanto, questions on if vaccinations are necessary or not, gay marriages being accepted throughout the United States, legalization of marijuana, no more animal cruelty being allowed or trophy hunting being accepted from all over the world... the list goes on.

We are no longer just a society filled with beliefs and obligations of old expectations thrust upon us. We are like adolescents becoming much more stimulated by challenges that we face together in order to become more independent. Rather than fearing challenges in these changing times, we are seeing that we do have a voice. The past no longer dictates the individual when the individual refuses to be dictated to.

BRAIN VS. MIND

A few months ago I was going on a business trip and was on a plane. The woman next to me was new to flying. As we ascended up into the lovely skies, she began to get chatty. Then she got extremely chatty – almost uncomfortable-like behavior. I figured she was nervous so I let her talk without interruption. I began to notice how she spoke of her mother and her friends. It didn't sound very happy. After about an hour of chatter and listening to negative talk, I couldn't help but to finally ask her if she'd seen the movie "Yes Man" with Jim Carrey. Her response was, "No, but is it like 'Liar Liar'?" I began to laugh and explained to her that sometimes we might need to go the extra mile and find a more productive way to help our relationships to possibly feel more joyful.

She had no clue that she was coming across negative, judgmental, and dissatisfied with choices she had made.

So, was her brain taking over with old patterns that were based on her insecurities, or was she looking for attention to feel better about herself, and possibly her vacation?

The distinction we really need to understand is that the mind is not necessarily the brain. As a matter of fact, the mind is much more than what the brain thinks. It's like the analogy of your brain being the flower, and the mind being the soil from the earth from which it grows.

In a recent article published by *Psychology Today* magazine, Bill Gordon, Ph.D. states that "the brain is part of the body, however the mind is a part of the transcendent world of wisdom and thought." He continues to say, "The mind's intelligence permeates every human cell, extending into the environment and carrying with it the wisdom of the ancients: social journey and kinship. The brain only connects the body; the mind connects all things. Pain communicates with the brain; suffering speaks to the mind."

So then, what this says to me is that we are much more than what we think! The mind then would include our deep desires, our heartfelt emotions, and our subconscious decisions lurking in the background waiting to be acknowledged. Maybe if we understood more about the mind, we could allow ourselves to comprehend more wisdom and compassion for it.

We are walking spirits making decisions daily by our actions. By recognizing this, we can empower ourselves to walk the "good red road" (a metaphorical expression from Native American Black Elk, Oglala Sioux medicine man) meaning living the spiritual way of life and staying on the right path. We can live purposefully and therefore, be responsible for our actions. The mind is filled with subconscious patterns that come to our conscious mind in order to be recognized, changed and redirected. If we realize we can change our thinking at any second, then we need to ask ourselves why we hold a specific idea or judgement in the first place? The answer is attachment.

As children, we don't know judgement. We know feelings. By attaching to those feelings, we sense the hurt, or a deep trauma that caused pain of some sort. No one ever told us it would be there forever if we held on to it. Instead, we have to learn how to release it at some point and move on.

We are beginning to see that we are living the "book of life" by surrendering to the knowledge that we simply do not know the big picture yet... it is for us to unravel and recreate in these wild times we live in. With as many astrological shifts and alignments that have been occurring in the most recent years, most of us can recognize more of this truth now. In the past, it would have seemed preposterous and too difficult to comprehend. We might have even thought that chaos, which creates bedlam, would supersede the foundation we thought we were here to create in the first place.

Whether we realize it consciously or not, we are already making differences every day in our higher frequency intention. Being in a state of wonder and pondering the bigger picture within you is spreading little fingers of consciousness throughout, and that's called humility. These are connective moments that are occurring in the space we live in... inside.

Our bodies feel this change more now than ever before; it's just not possible to exclude the body when we are experiencing dynamic expansion in these shifting times, after all. Our body is the physical result of the way we've lived our lives. It's like a computer that has used up its RAM, which is like the adrenal glands of our personal, physical system. Remission of illness is when we choose to allow life to burst through the old paradigm that we created through our thoughts, and that gives us more "RAM". We can defrag our own outdated material of thoughts and ways we used to think worked for us... sometimes just by realizing that we can let go and not hold on to anything simply for the sake of trying to hold it together.

I remember one time I had a friend that heard me going on about something that seemed so mundane to her, but not to me. Then she said, "Mona, if you died tomorrow, would that really be as important as you've decided it would be?" Wow - I had to hear that. I was sure my point was being overlooked... then I saw it. She was absolutely right. Why was I trying so hard? What was I actually hanging on to? Would anyone else at that time care about the personal attachment I was attributing to the situation? I doubted it, and rightfully so.

I think many times we as humans doubt our choices, our way of thinking, and even more so now that we are being unraveled. It's all part of the big picture, though, because the old ways just don't work anymore. We are just doing our best in trying to find our way.

As children, we are very astute in our ideas of forming our behavior patterns around our personality when we are faced with a situation which may become very uncomfortable. As life has it, we are very sensitive beings at an early age and feel more than we've given ourselves credit for. Some of us would say that we do not remember our childhood. However, this too could be a reaction to a sensitive time we had as a child. The difficult fact is that *not* remembering is just as much a part of the decision making as anything else we choose.

A lovely client of mine used to carry the burden of her grandmother's death, which happened when she was six years old. Her grandmother was the one who watched over her as a little one, and when she passed away, the little girl refused to speak for almost a year after. I read this information in her and she confirmed it. All of her life she carried the decision to not be all the way here on the planet, and began to live as though she was on the other side with her grandmother.

Needless to say, the rest of her life until now was reflecting the idea that somehow it was easier to live outside the body than in it. She ended up with many issues around this behavior identity, which lead to many sleepless nights, and while she experienced a heightened intuition, she never felt the love from Spirit; she always thought she was alone. Trust issues would arise from this, but the love she had for God kept her going. Today, she has realized this, and has mostly been able to shift a lifetime of "out of body" living to "it's nice to be able to trust life."

Our minds are asking to be understood as time continues to expand awareness within our soul. In some ways, it feels like our goal in this life is to achieve a level beyond our old perceptions that feels fulfilling, and only engage in choices that are acceptable to us. Our minds, however, are capable of mental shape shifting! We can think of several different things within seconds, and still drive a car not knowing how we got to our final destination. And yet, we continue to doubt ourselves.

If we can now realize that the subconscious mind is not a mystery but a tool to re-remember, or recognize, old patterns being put in our faces in order to ask ourselves if this is what we want or if these are the decisions we wish to make, etc. then we will welcome this in a new way and see that we are making our minds up: either based on old ideas and fears, or learning how big-spirited we truly are!

THE MIND'S MAGIC

I remember being enthralled with Harry Houdini as a kid, and always wanted to figure out how this man could make magic occur so easily while everyone was baffled.

Then years later I read a quote from him that seemed relevant to this particular part of the book. Houdini is quoted for saying, "My mind is the key that sets me free." To me this means his tricks had to seem real enough for him on some level for this magician to pull them off and create an astonished audience always wanting more. So, even though we are not Houdini, the mind works the same in all of us... how far are we willing to challenge ourselves to be set free?

A woman I worked on a while back made an appointment with me and asked if I could help her with an ongoing physical problem that the doctors and chiropractors couldn't diagnose to fix. I told her we could certainly give it a shot! So, she scheduled only a half hour with me because she was pretty skeptical. We talked over Skype, and as I looked at her, I could see that she was young and very bright! She was smart and educated, but very stuck.

As we began her session, she blew her nose and apologized for a cold she had developed a few days prior. In my energy world of working, we don't ignore those things. I explained to her that colds are not caught because of a virus necessarily, but you have to have the frequency of the cause itself inside of you in order to attract a cold. Some days we are certainly more vulnerable than others due to biorhythms and sensitivity. She understood.

I began to read more information from her and felt her pelvic region uptight and anxious. I asked her politely if she had difficulties in this area. It turned out not only did she, but I saw she had a tailbone issue that was "out of sync" and her lower parts were all thrown off physically. The tailbone was pushed high enough up so that every time she would sit down, she just couldn't stay put very long without pain, which also took her breath away. Her bladder was also affected. When the doctors did their diagnosis, they put her on meds, which actually made matters worse.

Being empathetic, I took her pain on for only a short time and read the reason for it through the feeling (when we hurt, it is actually a feeling speaking). I explained to her that this started several years ago when she was in college, and what I felt was at that time, she was in between colleges, somehow not being able to decide from one to the other. When I asked her if this was correct, she said, "Yes, but I didn't think that bothered me today." Back then, it created a decision that she later regretted in her life and wish she had chosen the other college. She admitted that if she had, this would have helped her with her job, her focus, and her direction later on. Interesting... so why did the tailbone become painful putting pressure on the bladder? (As a side note, when I do a talk, many people in the audience will raise their hands when I ask them, "Who fell on their tailbone when they were a kid before the age of 12"?)

First of all, the tailbone is related to deep rooted survival around family. Around the age of six, we question if we really have love or support as we experience living on this planet... especially from the people we feel should love us the most. And actually, in her case, it was that she didn't support her own decision and ignored her family completely. Bladder issues can be due to insecurity, nervousness, but mostly, questioning decisions around being too submissive or being angry. So "pressure" occurred as an indicator to help her recognize this had been there a long time and the pain body would only become more pressured until there was some form of relief. By sharing the truth of the read, she had relief and was able to see clearer in her world from then on.

Memories are like a physical weight. They're what weighs us down, makes us feel heavy, and causes a slew more effects that stop us from expansion.

FROM FEAR TO FREEDOM

Freedom is really nothing more than allowance. But how do we understand this?

For so many lifetimes, we learned behavior patterns because of fear. Every time we come back to this world, we once again have to decide how to recognize these patterns within us in order to consciously change them.

If you have ever experienced trauma, which most of us have, it's important to know that trauma memories usually become buried deep within us, until one day they erupt. They can cause changes in moods, outbursts of anger, submission, dislike of yourself, and the biggest one for SO many people is the fact that they feel they will never be good enough. I would say the majority of clients I have worked with over 40 years carry some form of trauma that controls the mind by a belief system that says, "When I am hurting in my heart, that's just natural" instead of, "I refuse to take someone's criticism of me personally and will live my own life."

Trauma memories, whether conscious or subconscious, continue to create reactions until they are recognized or reversed by taking responsibility and watching one's behavior. Does this mean the fear is a slave to memory? Or is the memory a slave to fear? We are usually a slave to the memory, and that means we are enslaved by events that no longer exist.

Learning to *use* our memories is much better than letting the memories use us.

So where does freedom of choice come in? Humans are creatures of habit, and usually find change scary or unwelcome as they build their daily lives based on their old patterns. Resistance can overpower or cloud our expansion (or freedom), and it's usually unconscious.

I have had several clients ask me what stops them from moving forward or manifesting their dreams? When I answer, the answers aren't always heard. Some people don't like what they hear, and yet these answers can be goldmines; the truth can really set you free! More than likely, subconscious fears and protection become insecurities and can stop us from feeling loved or abundant.

1. If you do not like yourself and do not feel abundant, write down 10 things that you DO like about yourself: things you have accomplished, or done for someone else. Did you do anything special for yourself recently?

2. When you were younger, did you ever feel you would never get what you wanted? Did you feel life would not allow you to have what you desired, or you weren't acceptable enough to get it? Sit down and recognize that, then begin to change it by telling yourself that is a false belief of the life you were, by right, meant to live. This is what is meant by "letting go."

3. Have you blamed others for your misfortune? Maybe a divorce had you feeling resentful, or you felt left out of family matters? These experiences can be holding back from creating an abundant life that can happen with the proper vibrational shifting. You just have to re-prioritize what takes priority in your mind, and then move on. **You** matter more than emotions that have held you back, and magic can occur spontaneously as you change that frequency.

EXPANSION IS QUANTUM

The longer I live and work in this glorious field of Medical Intuition, I see on a daily basis that whether you are old or young, big or small, nice or mean, happy or sad, you can change in a second. The body waits for you to become whole, real and honest within yourself. Have you noticed the people who are confident and funny, strong yet compassionate, are people who are leaders? They have learned the concept of balance. Jesus said, "The truth will set you free."

Each person I read hears a biofeedback of truth that is read in consciousness, which brings truth to recognition. It is always connection that creates a big bang effect, or what scientists call "zero point." This expands into a lovely effect called **freedom**.

We have many layers since we have lived many lives, and some people have actually recognized this and learned to the point where they are able to say, "Oh, that was me in a past life" if shown a picture of themselves in college, or even as a child. The growing mind lives in every cell of our body. Every memory, every moment, and each person we meet or encounter along the way trigger old emotions that become new with each encounter.

So, do we have choices in this life to see each of these as a lesson, a new experience, and even a change within ourselves to make a choice? Absolutely. We never again have to be a slave to a memory that is dead and gone. By old memories being triggered, we can expand our sense of feeling within our heart as a tiny shift, taking a frown to a smile, or even saying something encouraging instead of demeaning. The best part about these choices is that it changes everything that has existed within our DNA and begins a healing for strands that were frayed. It can reverse the process and bring you to a joyful state again. The effects of something so simple can:

1. Release stress

2. Change your patterns
3. Lower blood pressure
4. Grow stamina
5. Stop mood swings
6. Help irrational feelings become rational
7. Keep you healthier
8. Change your eating habits
9. Help you feel lighter
10. And even create confidence

Bruce Lipton, a global speaker, cellular biologist, visionary, author, and friend, says we have seven trillion cells in our body and each cell is a battery. Inside each cell is a negative charge and outside the cell is a positive charge. That means we have seven trillion volts of energy going through us every second of every day. Encouraged by the heart, we make the choices of just how vibrantly these cells can interact, or not. Worry, expectations, holding grudges, are all unnecessary stresses that pop these feelings into priority, putting the adrenals high on the meter of the fight or flight mode. Constantly protecting yourself will decrease your sleep, keep you stuck, make your energy levels drop, and not let you make a confident decision. Some people continually get migraines for these reasons, and that is simply due to the protective pattern.

Expansion of the mind must be recognized as trusting life itself. Flexibility is the "F" word to some, yet it is the way to balance the psyche and, coming back to allowance, will set us free.

CHAPTER TWO
~ YOUR HEART'S DIVINE PURPOSE ~

My favorite thing to read in a body when I do my work is information from the heart. It can never lie, and actually the heart is released from a stronghold of emotion when it has support. The client actually feels a sense of lightheartedness! Their breathing gets deeper, which then clears any foggy brain, and they noticeably feel a change in their psyche. In this quantum change, it's the connection to truth that is mostly responsible, but also the intention to heal. A person must want to feel better and help their life experiences get easier as well. Again, the old statement "where two or more are gathered" comes to mind!

This chapter could be the whole book. The heart is a magnificent organ, and so very much more! Our heart beats about 60 to 100 times a minute. In each of these moments we have the ability to produce a whole new perception of life, our bodies, and new concepts related to anything we choose.

It's quite amazing to know that we can change our own blood pressure by releasing the brain's interpretation of stress. However, not many of us can actually do that very quickly. The reality is definitely there though. The Institute of HeartMath in Boulder Creek, California tells us that in the science of the heart, we are all connected to each other, to nature, and even to the universe. They even have a device called the Em-Wave to help you be more conscious about your heart rhythm variable (HRV) and how to rest the heart from stress.

There are YouTube videos featuring Rollin McCraty, the Science Director of the Global Coherence Initiative, that help you to further understand how the Em-Wave is a tool for everyone to help make better choices in life. Rollin also has many books about intuition, which comes from the heart. His latest one is called *Science of the Heart*, which is an exploration of studies done at the Institute of HeartMath. It teaches us about energetic communication and intuition research. This is what coherence means, along with the importance of it in our lives.

Then in astrology, we learn what our individual charts tell us about ourselves from the moment we are born. Astrology is a study of the movements of the planets that have a definite influence on human affairs, as well as the design of each person's life choices. This is why we are born under a certain sign.

There are different types of astrology used to help interpret someone's life course, goals, love life, etc. Many astrologers today agree that we are in intense times, as planets and their influences have contributed to things such as earthquakes, storms, illnesses, etc. Ironically, they agree that ultimately you are in charge of your life, your lessons, and your future. Astrology just sets the stage for you to help make those decisions. The electromagnetic changes in the Earth's atmosphere affect the hearts and minds of humanity, however we are the drivers of our own cars.

I love science. It truly gives us the measurements of our own productivity in the magnetic fields of the Earth and the body. And yet, how will that help us when we are experiencing a difficult time? How does this come in handy when we are dealing with abuse or raising a difficult child? The answer is: the more you know, the more you learn, and the more prepared you are through understanding, the better you will feel in the long run over the decisions you make for yourself and everyone involved. The tools I've mentioned will certainly come in handy, however you are the creator: the conscious being that makes life happen, and the universe within. Therefore, you are what it takes for our world to function, to develop, and to express. Whether it be through silence or through voicing an opinion, you are the magic that creates, moment by moment.

The heart is the only place where you truly change to help the mind become more expanded in life itself. It is the only organ that does not get cancer. In my work, I have witnessed so many incredible people and seen many outcomes without any of them being good or bad. The heart does not judge. Cause and effect are natural, however even the heart becomes clouded by blockages that came in from past lifetimes, or false interpretations as we were being raised. In other chapters, I will explain placebo, nocebo, and even help with guided meditations to personally show you the power of the heart.

I have rarely seen two people alike that make the exact same decisions based on one circumstance. Everyone has an idea they reflect on based from an experience they encountered at some point in their lives.

When I hear people ask me about why they are having trouble attracting a partner, money, a good job, etc., it's easy to say the same thing many other speakers and healers see and say. However, I have learned that there is more to the story.

Over a period of several years, I not only heard of the electromagnetic field around the body, but would see auras if the lights were dim enough. "Prana", a very light, vibrant, auric energy about an inch to two thick immediately surrounding a body, is all that voltage shining right outside of it. If you turn the lights down low and go where there is a mirror (bathrooms are always good for this), you can see it. This is a part of the electromagnetic energy in the field. Science is very clear not to call this field an "aura". They are scientists and must measure it for different reasons.

Being a HeartMath trainer and mentor myself, the science of the heart teaches us that no one field is larger than another, but it can be brighter when we are happy vs. when we are sad. The field is what attracts and detracts energy or relationships, etc. because it is all stimulated from your heart. Your heart will generate the field, and that is how people can detect if they instantly like each other or not. The field is then responsible for the energy and the frequencies it puts out.

It's like if you were to walk into a room... you would notice the chairs, the windows, wallpaper, tables, etc. But due to who has been in there before, you may notice once you walk in that you feel good, calm, light, or it could be the opposite. I've been known to walk out of a room or building because of the energy. Crystal shops, restaurants, book stores, grocery stores, etc. have felt like nails on a chalkboard at times. The heart's generative abilities will give you feedback, but not everyone is as sensitive. Certain energies can be adaptable, and others are not acceptable.

The field is amazing! It carries energies you came into this world with from past lives, called carry-overs. These energies don't leave you, but they *are* mutable. We can change these once we learn higher lessons and become conscious of our decisions. The brain will try to interpret a quick decision automatically, simply based on past experiences. The amygdala in the brain is one of four basal ganglia in each cerebral hemisphere that is part of the limbic system and looks like an almond shaped mass of grey matter near the temporal lobe. Fancy words for a tiny piece of matter that holds on to memory as a protective shield without mercy! This is why, when the brain signals an experience, it's because of an attachment somewhere from the moment there was a shock to you - a quick trauma, a non-forgiving format - that made an impact to the heart.

A deep hurt, such as losing a child or a loved one, or even a divorce, can continue to live deep within us, which can eventually cause an autoimmune dysfunction such as cancer, Multiple Sclerosis, Parkinson's, or even Alzheimer's. These diseases have their own recognition to the pain of the past, though, which is why they are different.

So, does this mean our heart is dysfunctional? Absolutely not. Our belief system is. That is why we are here, to learn a new way of listening, of interpreting a cause to an effect, and even a new way of developing our brain to get out of the jail (or stronghold) it was once safe in as it was following orders. Now we can learn the truth and can learn a better way to see clearer without the blockages that were once our survival.

THE SPIRITUAL IMMUNE SYSTEM

Recently I have enjoyed being on many radio shows and it felt like I was channeling information about how the body works. It came down to what I call the "Spiritual Immune System", which needs our attention if we shall ever change our health on every - or any - level. Emotional, mental, spiritual, and physical ailments can be seen from a different perspective that isn't so personal, but profound.

Not only is the heart a powerful source of wisdom, creation, and knowledge, but it is where we delve into our higher selves, which is our soul. We incarnate many times in this world, coming back each time with a sense of purpose. However, the purpose we seek is not always the purpose we are to live. Purpose isn't about what job you do, or how many kids you are "supposed" to have, etc.

Joseph Campbell, a well-known American professor of literature and well-loved teacher of myths, legends, and spiritual concepts around these topics and religion, has stated truths like, "follow your bliss" and told a metaphysical story loved by many today called *The Hero's Journey*, which I shared in my last book. He helped make the understanding of the word, "purpose" simple by stating that, "smiling at a child can be a purpose." What it comes down to is this: purpose is creation instigated by the heart to promote an expression of passion and drive. We all have free will, and what we do with that is the larger reason we exist: to create for love.

It truly is in the wisdom of the heart that we can take off and experience just as much joy as we do educating ourselves to a higher degree of living.

So, the "Spiritual Immune System" is a derivative of our own heart. You see, we have a magnetic field around us, which is scientifically proven to react from the feelings you have initiated throughout time. This field reflects itself to everything, and causes you to attract or detract experiences to learn from; also to enjoy. So, you might say it is a teacher to your world. What you attract is in the energy that you create and put out. When you change a simple feeling, or learn a technique, such as Ho'oponopono from the Hawaiian way of life "living from aloha", then you change the energetic magnitude of the field. In HeartMath we say, "what are you feeding the field?"

The good news is that when you become more open to possibilities without fear or discomfort, you grow in your ability to become more intuitive. Basically, an expansion occurs, yet your field doesn't change in size. It changes in magnitude. Nikola Tesla said, "If you want to find the secrets of the universe, think in terms of energy, frequency, and vibration." In many forms of shamanism, this is the only way the language is. That's because to make the best decisions for the tribe, a shaman must listen to the feelings of the heart. They must feel the vibration of the moment, the connection without fear, and the clarity of love (always in the moment for that divine connection). I'd like to think that this is how we can all be, act, and teach.

Your "Spiritual Immune System" will be the reflector of your thoughts and the lessons learned as well. I love the vastness of constant allowance of interpretation as the mind is boggled with the passion for freedom. To think that all of this is within reach, and that the heart clearly loves to breath, to feel connected, and the brain waves become more alive with energy as we allow the heart to unveil even more of the wisdom it knows to be true, versus the survival of subconscious thoughts that stop us from living.

Our health depends on this wisdom.

What are some of the ways we can look into our hearts for peaceful reassurance?

1. Trust yourself. You can never really learn to grow without experiencing something, no matter how big or small. Recognize that when we judge a decision before we actually make it, we can keep feeling stuck and then we end up not making the decision that will benefit us in the long run.

2. Learn that when you resonate to music, laughter, and good vibes of any kind, you are receiving. We must remember that the giving and receiving of emotions are like the ebb and flow of the ocean. We only leave behind what no longer serves us.

3. Other people have different experiences and lessons. Taking on someone else's feelings or pain can hurt you. Everyone is an empath, but to different degrees. No one needs to believe they are over sensitive and helpless. We honor others when we become compassionate, not judgmental. Letting people, no matter who they are, learn their own lessons can be difficult, yet this is what is known as "Unconditional Love". This goes for everyone.

4. Take time for yourself. Our busy schedules get busier and patterns are formed as cycles continue. All of this is changeable, mutable and can be more consciously directed. In doing so, we then create better, have more stamina, and definitely less stress!

5. Go the extra mile. If you feel like you are stuck, be courageous and do something different. Your heart will guide you as you recognize signs that are being given to you by the universe. All of this is coming from "permission of the heart".

6. Someone else's belief system is not yours. You create whatever you want. My saying that I quote often is, "We're makin' all of this up!" Therefore, if we created it, we can change it. By challenging your own beliefs, you find a way out of the past.

7. You are not a victim. The heart will direct you (through intuition) towards a reaction to any action and lead you to the outcome. Judging an outcome stops your creativity from getting a chance to blossom.

All of the above statements are available any time for your heart to feel the awareness of the moment. For THIS is the divine mission of the heart: to keep you balanced in all areas of your life without insecure motives falsely leading you astray.

Knowing that the past is over and a new day calls for a new beginning, our perceptions now have the opportunity to become alive, surprising ourselves through spontaneity, and giving us a gift anytime we choose to receive it. Love is truly all there is. When we contemplate anything, it is a form of meditation. There is nothing "wrong" with looking at a situation and wondering about an action you created, or the possibility of a problem arising. However, catch yourself if you feel this to be harmful, and recognize as the observer that you are learning, not judging. As a music lover, I love the song by John Lennon called, "Watching the Wheels".

In the words pertaining to perceptions, he sings:

"Ah, people ask me questions,
Lost in confusion.
Well I tell them there's no problem,
Only solutions.

Well they shake their heads and look at me, as if I lost my mind.
I tell them there's no hurry, I'm just sitting here doing time."

What better way to explain truth? We are all sitting here doing time, so what are we doing with that time? There really are no problems, only solutions. I heard this song when I was a child and decided I would do my best to live by this wisdom. The trick is to just enjoy our time, which takes time to learn.

Singer-songwriter James Taylor writes:

"The secret of love is enjoying the passage of time.
Any fool can do it, there ain't nothin' to it...
The secret of love is in opening up your heart.
It's ok to feel afraid, but don't let it stand in your way.
Everyone knows that love is the only road...

The thing about time is that time isn't really real.
It's all on your point of view.
How does it feel to you?
Einstein said he could never understand it all.
Planets spinning through space,
The smile upon your face,
Welcome to the human race...

It's just a lovely ride"

ANOTHER LESSON OF THE FIELD

I have seen many children with horrific challenges, such as Cerebral Palsy, MS, early stroke and heart difficulties resulting in several surgeries, Rheumatoid Arthritis, as well as many other autoimmune dysfunctions. Many of these wonderful children who came into this world with these challenges were born here in order to teach, or to become more whole from a carry-over in a past life. These cases for energy work are profound and the children love their sessions. However, some are very sensitive, almost to the extreme of throwing up after the session.

One day I worked on a little girl with many challenges, which I read was definitely a carry over. She was only five years old in this life, but her energetic story was that she was an old woman in her past life and had not finished what she came here to do.

I read that she was a go-getter personality and didn't want to stop working for good causes, which came with determination. In her past life, she had completely overdone it and had no energy left by the time she passed away. As an infant in this life, interestingly enough, she developed a stroke at eight months old. This left her partially immobile physically, which is what the parents wanted to help her heal from. The stroke caused many more physical ailments, impatience, and physical challenges, as well as a very sensitive heart and extreme sensitivity to life.

One day as I worked with her, I noticed she began to get very ill. She began to express emotions like anger and temper tantrums. She wasn't behaving at all and would even throw food. It was like her personality was changing with the energy work! This was highly unusual because many people, children, and even animals of all kinds, respond with peace. Most will fall asleep or need a nap shortly after the session. However, this was not the case with this little girl. This, of course, fascinated me. I had to know why she was reacting with such strong, explosive emotion, inside and out.

As I read and connected to her energy, I saw it to be almost "invasive" to do healing work with her because she was too young to actually give permission, so the parents and I worked together. Her reactions were due to feeling that she wanted to be grown up, and her frustration was so obvious. Strangely, she considered this feeling of healing energy in her body a threat. It was almost like she wanted to take control of her life and the heck with guides, healers, or anyone wanting to help her!

I decided to give her space and explained to the parents that all healing work must have permission from the one receiving it, and also to do no harm. They listened intently but could not move past wanting to help her. They asked again, because even with her form of strong reaction, she seemed to be doing better in the quiet moments. I admired the parents. They were humble and only wanting the best for their child, as any loving parent would.

About a month later, we tried again, however this time I didn't want to be intrusive to her body, so my guidance told me to go into the field instead. I did just that. I ran the energy around the body, not in it. I was able to see the divots and weak spots in the field as I read her history. This was a **whole new way** to do special healing work.

Diverting from the normal way of working in the body, I found that this gave the field a boost and released her past a bit better, therefore giving her more joy around current moments. Within a few months her digestion seemed better, she was more creative, talkative, and clearer about how she perceived her life. As a child we can sometimes be more directive with a personality when it comes to past lives and actions than we can as adults. Adults have already accepted life as it was in the field. That's why we can change anything if we realize the heart and the moment matter more than any other thing.

So how does our electro-magnetic energy field represent the law of attraction? The word vibration in the dictionary means, "Electromagnetic wave; an oscillation of the parts of a fluid, or an elastic solid whose equilibrium has been disturbed; a person's emotional state or atmosphere, as communicated to, or felt by others."

When it comes to our own electro-magnetic field, it is constantly moving and fluctuating. Energy never stands still. It will carry a vibration until you connect to it and shift it. It takes a conscious decision, courage, and mostly recognition to a reaction you carry to a situation, or a little extra time out from your other thoughts. This can happen as we discover there is always perfect timing in an "A-HA" moment. If we hear a song on the radio that is in that "perfect timing" to something or someone you just thought of, then this is another form of deep connection without trying. It's the intensity of that thought or memory that has more juice to produce a physical or cosmic reaction in our own individual worlds. To know that we can change these intensities or deep-seated emotions is where the power's at.

CHAPTER THREE
~ COMING TO YOUR SENSES ~

"Nothing can cure the soul but the senses, just as nothing can cure the senses... but the soul." - Oscar Wilde

The word itself, "sense", has a wide variety of usages: a sense of time, or common sense, or even the mind! This one is interesting because it's an internal sense that can create its very own stimuli in and through thought forms. The dictionary meaning of the word "sensation" attributes to a physical feeling or perception as a result of something that comes into contact with the body (that's why to know thyself is to use thy senses!). Perceptions of sound come through the ears, and the perceptions of the mind come through mental chatter. It's amazing how even dreams can concur with this as we can visualize so many things in a dream state.

What this boils down to is awareness. Senses are a very big part of our body because they actually balance us with feelings and remind our spirit of tender moments and nostalgic memories. They also warn us when danger is near, as our skin gets goosebumps and our hair stands on end. Without our senses, we couldn't gauge direction, or sense boundaries, or even more profound, comprehend vision to make important decisions.

Our senses are so critical, yet if we lose one, or are born with only a few, those working senses get stronger. I knew a blind man who listened to every move going on around him in order to gauge his distance from the street, the curb, and knew where he was going. There was also a blind gent several years ago that I saw on a newscast that clicked with his mouth when he rode a bicycle. As we can see, not having a sense only leads to better and stronger sensing, like the dolphin uses its echolocation for sound navigation.

Senses are not in concrete by any means, as nothing in the body ever is. I went to see Deepak Chopra in 2018, as I had seen him 20 years prior. I am always mesmerized by his knowledge and comprehension of science and the body. The quote that I loved the most was, "The body is an activity." Everything he mentioned after that fell into this idea. I work with this awesome comprehension as I work with clients every day and can confirm the truth of this statement. For this is how the body operates and co-operates! It's definitely through our desires and realities.

We know we are spirits in our physical form, and actually, we create this physical form with our deep internal thoughts and feelings. The body always works together, like a well-oiled machine, unless there is a blockage of flow, or incorrect information that we are living by that does not adhere to our soul. What that means is programming from parents, peers, teachers, religion, or any meaningful acceptance that wasn't truly "up your alley", has thrown your sail a bit off course and had you searching for land. This is why we feel stuck a lot.

We reach these points in our lives where we feel deep down that there has to be more to living. This is actually good! It helps us reach out of our comfort zone and explore. If we can do that without judging ourselves and feel the freedom to live outside the box (the box being the old thought patterns of the brain) and realize we are the creators of our brain waves, then we will become happy in ourselves and much more aware in our daily lives to increase our manifestation and learn to live heaven on Earth.

Our senses will keep us on track, as long as we listen and use them. It's the heart that is the captain, and the senses are the crew. The fun part about knowing that is that you can actually change what you want when you want.

Let's take something simple. You are looking at a vase of flowers that you picked from your garden. You admire the vase because it came from Aunt Martha. Then you observe the flowers. You witness the colors, the fragrance, and the life span. All together it makes you happy to witness that these came from your garden, so a sense of pride comes over you. Now, if you are in a bad mood because you and your partner had an argument, are you picking these flowers to try to help you feel better or are you doing it for your partner? At any rate, the message is to *stay in the moment* and recognize your feelings, then you can shift in a second just by allowing the flowers to be there, speak to your heart, and then get back on track.

The senses are there for us to connect back to the heart, or is the heart connecting to us through our senses?

Here is an exercise that you might want to engage in by reading it out loud and then recording it. Most cell phones have a recorder app you can use for this purpose:

As I sit here quietly in my comfortable place, I
realize I am not just in my body, but in every part of
my mind and my being.
Breathing in and out I recognize that I am in the
moment, and very capable of going anywhere I want
with my eyes closed.
My senses work for me whether I am somewhere
else or right here in my comfortable place.
Today, I will decide to go to the beach.
I am now laying on the sand in a tropical paradise
with a beach towel and the beverage of my choice.
I give myself a moment to see what is all around me.
I listen to the sounds of what is here, as there are
many sounds at once.
I breathe in and can smell the ocean air.
I can even taste the salty air as the gentle winds
blow my way, cooling off the heat on my body.
The birds are chirping as if to talk to me.
I can hear the ocean crashing up on the rocks not
far away, and my heart is so happy.
I am in Paradise.
I find that I am thirsty.
I am taking a sip from my delicious cold beverage
and can taste the flavors of the ingredients.
I find this to be so refreshing.
The temperature of the drink is perfect.
I feel the wind back on my face and am grateful for
the breeze.
Suddenly I get a whiff of a nearby tree with a
fragrance that reminds me of when I was a child.
What am I smelling?
The clouds are coming in from the West and I feel
it's time to gather my belongings and go back.
I will come back here anytime I choose
to experience this divine moment.

My senses are grateful.
My heart is peaceful.

You can do this exercise repeatedly, and it is quite amazing to be able to really "sense" the beach and all of the qualities of this experience! I do this exercise for retreat clients and each one has a different experience. This is known as a guided meditation. I love these!

When I was in high school, I remember the teacher had to step out for an emergency. I found it interesting that she asked me to "watch the class" until she got back. I walked up to her desk and in front of all the juniors and seniors, I asked if they would like to try something fun. No arguments from the peanut gallery! So, I had them move all the chairs and lay down on the floor or sit comfortably against the wall. I thought it would be nice if they were grounded. Then we started.

I said, "Take off your shoes, get comfortable, and close your eyes." I dimmed the lights in the room and proceeded to guide them in to any place they felt they wanted to go where there was a rose. Some chose gardens, others chose a vase on the mantle in their homes, and some just only saw a rose. Then I began: "What color is it? Is it a bud or is it open? What size is it? Does the stem have thorns or is it smooth? How do you feel about this rose? What kind of smell does it have? Can you smell this rose?"

When the teacher got back, she thought there was a hippie infestation! She asked me, "Mona, I put you in charge. What is this?" I explained that I was doing an experiment to see if these kids would comply, and then we could discuss what they saw." She liked it, so we continued to ask questions from the students to see what they had seen or experienced. Much to our surprise, every one of them loved this. They said they really felt this rose, smelled it, tuned in to it, and some were very graphic. I found that the color they chose related to their personality. One student said it was a black rose and sat up on the mantle in a lonely vase. When I asked her if it had a smell to it, she said yes, and much to her surprise, it was like lilac. So, I took each student's info and wrote out what the colors meant, and how this was an interpretation of their life... from the perspective of a rose.

The girl with the black rose thanked me afterwards and said she was always alone. Her parents worked and she would come home from school every day to an empty house. She was studious, but lonely. She didn't have brothers and sisters, so she had to keep herself occupied until her parents would come home. She was so smart. When she asked me what all that meant, I explained that she was ALL colors in one personality (some interpretations indicate this is a color related to mourning. Even though it can be, the perception of every color in black puts a positive spin on this).

I told her being alone isn't always bad. It brings out your creative flow and gets your mind active to desires, and therefore you are more flexible than other people - and black is flexible! She smiled and said thank you. Then I laughed and told her how often I was alone after school, which is how I came up with this exercise. Walking home from school every day in Southern California wasn't too bad. I enjoyed the observation of how I felt walking by a tree with a special scent, or different flowers blooming, and watched how each day there were even more flowers. Later in life when I walked anywhere, I always looked for blooming plants and trees. (To this day, I still do, and my appreciation for these is still excites me!)

That awesome, simple exercise can be done for you or for a loved one. Guided meditations can bring out information and can be changed anytime. There are various forms of color that resonate a different frequency and can even change your mood. This is why when you pick out an outfit, you will typically pick one with a hue that matches you! Some psychologists are finding new discoveries of information with their patients and use this form of therapy with specific cases.

Here is my list of some of our special colors and how they affect the body:

Yellow: Yellow is a derivative of gold, yet the color has a different vibe all together. Yellow gives a feeling of peace, but it also has a high vibration of joy. It gives a non-invasive sensation that all is well. We can actually meditate on this color if it's raining too much outside and our mood becomes cranky or disillusioned. Colors are biofeedback, so concentration on these colors helps to naturally recreate your mood.

Gold: Gold is the highest frequency there is in the form of a color. It has the power to transcend any emotion, any situation, and be clear and strong for your innate desire for love and for strength. It is the color vibration of your higher self. By focusing on gold, you transcend even the need for money, and yet you can become more aware by using the intention to help you manifest in general. Jesus is pictured with a gold aura in many cases to show the vibrancy of the essence of the Creator. If you can imagine a shimmering gold around you and pay attention to how your mind is accepting that, you could potentially shift any situation. Gold doesn't need acceptance. It just is and does.

Blue: There are many shades of blue, but the utmost purpose is to keep balance in your life. Some psychologists say that blue is transparent and adapts to your spiritual senses. It is good to feel your reaction to it and see which form of blue resonates to your liking. Dark blues are deep with a sense of trust, loyalty, sincerity, heaven, and peace from the depths. Light blues are non-threatening and can create a sense of joy to the heavens (hence, blue sky).

Green: Green is simply friendly and approachable. Many people associate green to nature. It's a safe color, and one that is loved for how it feels so healing. As a matter of fact, the heart chakra (energy field) is green, and symbolizes health, prosperity and abundance.

Orange: Orange is an amazing color. Some people can't take it too long, or don't like it. We eat oranges, which make us feel refreshed, light, happy, and oranges have many nutrients. The color itself is related to warmth, joy, enthusiasm, success, fun, sexuality, expression, freedom and so on. This is a great color to bring about more creativity.

Purple: A very popular color, purple enhances and enriches our spirituality and helps with confidence, expansion of awareness, connection to higher consciousness, and deep empowerment. Some say it balances your soul's desire to your body, creating a union of connection (not a bad idea to try focusing on this color at least five minutes a day and see if you feel a difference after about five days). I have seen purple reassure people in times of panic and give a sense of hope.

Pink: Pink is simply delicious for anyone who knows the playful part of your spirit! It keeps the vibration high, but not strong. Pink is recognized as love, passion, forgiveness, joy, appreciation, compassion, and as they say in Hawaii, "No worries."

Brown: You wouldn't guess this necessarily, but brown is classy. It suggests grounding, earth, wood, honesty, stability, pleasure, healing, security and it can actually stimulate the senses! As neutral as it is, it has the ability to promote taking that next step forward. Motivation, depth, and strength can come from this color, especially when you wear it.

Red: Red is a pretty deliberate color with pure intention. When it is visible, red is at extremes. Its powerful force can indicate life force (blood), anger, seduction or deep passion, and adventure into the unknown. If it's a lighter shade, it can mean love. As the color of fire, red is also purification.

Sometimes we can sense when danger is near, and we can be urged to react. We'll notice our heartbeat quickens, and our adrenals go into fight or flight. This response can occur in the body the same as any other sense. However, this is an innate feeling that is troublesome, and the hair can still stand up on the back of your neck. Paying attention is the key.

I have a story about a man I worked on about 20 years ago. He seemed a bit off, like he was not tracking. He was referred to me by a psychologist who loved my work and thought I could help this guy. However, she didn't tell me the whole truth about him because of client confidentiality. I noticed he was very quiet. When I asked him what he came to see me for, he said his psych doctor suggested it. I told him he didn't have to stay if he was uncomfortable. "No," he said, "I don't want to disappoint her." So, I had him go into the room and at that time, I was reading the essence of my clients through hands-on massage. He took a while to get on the massage table, and each time I asked him if he was ready, he'd say, "Just a minute."

One minute lead to the next and I couldn't wait any longer. I opened the door and he was standing there fully clothed looking at my belongings in the room, like the lamp, the card holder, the dream catcher, etc. One more time I asked him if he wanted to do this, and he said yes, he was just admiring my things. He got on the table and just took off his shirt. My instincts were telling me that he was not right.

Then it happened. The minute I laid my hands on his left leg, I got a spiritual shock run through my body. It felt like a shock wave of a different reality. Suddenly I saw a vision that included a murder. Even though I kept working, I saw splashes of red everywhere and then a woman who resembled what his mother might look like. I took a chance and asked him some questions. The psychologist told him I was able to read energy and help repair the body, the mind, etc. so I had to be careful, but I asked him if he was going to be taking a trip soon. His answer was as I expected, and yes, he was going to see his mother. I asked where she lived, and he said California. I picked up San Diego since I saw the area of Hotel Coronado. I was getting confirmation of where he might attack his mother just in case. I warned the psychologist and she assured me she would approach this and help in her own way as well (the color red was very intense in this case).

I love Edgar Cayce, the famous and wonderful psychic of the 40's, who talks about the power of color as well as the energy vibrations of crystals and stones.

Many shamans and healers use these tools to help calm the body or create a sense of peace or power to influence the psyche of the patient. I have used these therapies for years.

If you have used essential oils, flower essences, or any other vibrational therapy, chances are you sensed what was best for you and were drawn to the ones with potent results.

Bruce Lipton, author of *Spontaneous Evolution, Biology of Belief,* and *The Honeymoon Effect* says that we must remain mindful. That is **not** the same as thinking all the time. Mindful is being present in the moment and consistent with that as much as possible in order to recognize your thoughts, desires, decisions, etc. We are in a virtual reality suit called the body. Therefore, we are individual broadcasting systems, like a TV. Even if the TV is off, does that mean the signal is not there? We can turn it on anytime we want to, to any channel (perception) we want, and then broadcast it back into the field. We can then smell that rose, taste that chocolate, and see that sunset. The choice is ours.

As human creators, or co-creators, the world is filled with challenges, discoveries, and much beauty. If we can all remember the importance of this, we will open the senses to discover that life comes first.

I remember reading the bible as a kid, and sometimes certain phrases come back with more meaning today than at the time I first read them. The biblical phrase, "Where two or more are gathered, so there shall I be" (Matt 18:20), suggests that the connection of *anything* becomes biofeedback, and that itself is creation. For example, if I say something to you, and you say something back, it's communication *and* it's also biofeedback! It gives you an emotional response or a thought process, etc. It's more than physical because we are also listening. It's also how we accept something... similar to what a beautiful song can do for us. This is also how we listen, learn and feel.

Everything we see and pay attention to is a focus, and when we get an answer or a result, that in itself is a form of biofeedback. Sound is another good example. Cymatics (the study of modal vibrational phenomena) produces a physical shape and design when attributed to a tone in a plate of sand. Biofeedback, then, is a result of melding energy where one entity offers something and the other receives it. Manifestation is, therefore, also biofeedback.

A while back, I read a phrase from a book that was about life after death. The person who wrote it had a near-death experience. She stated that it is actually the small things you do in life, simply because you want to, that make a huge impact in the afterlife. It's not that you get an A+ each time you give a dollar to a homeless person, it is what it does to your feelings and your heart, which generates more love. It's that *internal motivation* that feeds the soul with pleasure and guides us to creating new motivations because our senses pick up on the feeling.

CONNECTING TO THE INNER-NET

Everybody is intuitive. If you have a heart, and it's beating, then you have intuition. If you think you don't, and many people have said they don't "sense" anything, it just means your antennae are down and you haven't given much time to allow yourself to pay attention to it. This is why it's so good to have quiet time! Also, as a key point, expectations are not intuition. Expectations are simply that. The frequency of expectation is lower than sensing a feeling because it can involve worry, anxiety, and stops a proper outcome from occurring, therefore creating a blockage in the flow. Impulses are not intuition either, as they are thrusts without clear intention and are not always in our favor. However, a sudden force that impels an instinct is known as an "inherent impulse", and that alone can change an action or behavior.

Studies show that the heart knows what will happen minutes before the event occurs. In the studies done at the Institute of HeartMath, they have hooked people up to sensors to examine their heartbeats, brain waves, etc. These people were then exposed to pictures of animals, and other random pictures such as scenery, and even a few musical instruments, parachuting, and so on.

They were asked to watch a blank screen for six seconds, and the computer randomly selected one of these photographs for three seconds. Then they were asked to hit a button and begin the process again, repeating about 30 times. After analyzing all the data, the results were astounding. The heart seemed to know the images *before* the participants ever saw the picture with their eyes. If the future picture was going to be something considered sad, the heart rate would drop five seconds before the randomly selected images actually showed up. The heart rate would react with a quickening if the picture was shocking, but always five seconds before the actual picture showed.

Labs all around the world have done these studies and this indicates the sensors are already within us. There has also been proof that the heart knows first, *then* the info goes to the brain, and *then* the body. In other words, when we get a "gut" feeling, it was actually addressed in the heart before it reached the gut.

Think about that moment when you got a call from someone you were just thinking about. Random? Or (and this one everyone loves) knowing you would get that parking place you were looking for and then bam - it opened up.

As you can see, the more we use this skill, or pay attention to it, it will deliver effects. It's like anything else that you spend time doing. When we go to school, we need to study to understand the subject a bit better. Same goes for our internal perceptions. It doesn't matter what religion you are or the family you grew up in. This lovely mechanism is natural. If you had a partner at one time who you knew wasn't the best for you but you chose them anyway, there were subconscious lessons for learning that you chose to experience. It's not a matter of judging, it's a matter of learning. As with all life lessons, growth is in the action, the reaction or the non-action. It is also in the "two steps forward, one step back" concept, until we go those two steps forward and **no** steps back.

Again, this becomes the biofeedback that is necessary to listen to; we make the same "mistake" all over again until we recognize that we are in charge and make our own decisions.

The body will always sense things by hair standing up, a tingle, ringing in the ears, or even a mother's intuition. Senses are our connection to the soul, and to each other. Albert Einstein is known for his amazing mind, and one of his famous quotes says, "The only real valuable thing in life is intuition."

Neale Donald Walsch, author of *Conversations with God* says, "An intuitive statement is one that you know is true even before you know why or how it is true."

When you become more connected to your own alignment within the heart, change can become immediate. We can develop more of our sense of knowing when we allow the energy, we listen to from the inside become more apparent. That's why we can create what we truly desire - not by trying to make it happen, but by creating from the inside out. The early childhood programming needs to be confronted to a degree to be able to change. Life has a way of showing us when it is time to grow, to accept a new challenge, and to trust that little voice inside that can turn into a big voice.

Many years ago, I was going through a divorce. It was not easy of course, because having three children and feeling responsible for my actions, my job, and mostly how this was going to affect our lives in the long run no matter what age my children were, threw me into a tizzy. Where I lived at the time was not working for me and my gut feeling was to move and to do it quickly. So, I found a little house, and when I moved out, my psyche began to change. (Stress can do that too, and depending on your choices, it can transpire new ideas when you hit the wall, or it can devastate you and create more experiences for learning.)

It was late August in 1999 and my mother was to come see me in October. As I was taking it a day at a time and realizing that my birthday was coming up, I had a funny feeling come over me to call my mom. I called her very late one night, and she lived in Michigan. I lived in Oregon, so the time difference was significant. However, my mom answered the phone and said, "Hi honey! Are you ok?" I began to cry and told her that I was not doing too well and was sorry that I was calling so late. She just laughed and said, "Don't worry about that. You can call me anytime." We chatted about my situation and agreed we'd see each other in October. In the meantime, I knew she would call me on my birthday, as she had done every year. But this time, I didn't get a call. Instead, a gut-wrenching feeling came over me and I knew something wasn't right.

My sister called a day later and said my mom had gone into the hospital and had to have a procedure to help her esophagus to help open her airway. As it turned out, when she was to come see me, she was having a pacemaker put in. Without my sister calling me, I knew she had crossed over. I felt my heart sink and sensed I needed to help her cross. I felt her so strongly and knew the communication was beyond words, beyond conscious comprehension, and that I was with her when she was crossing over.

When my sister called to tell me the news, it was like hearing it for the first time - which it was, verbally - but my heart knew. This is where our real connection to each other comes into play, without judgements or discomforts, but the true essence of being. Intuition is more than the word identifies with. It's **knowing**. The more we do it, the more we live it. And the better we get at it!

12 weeks later, I had a dream that my dad was calling me, and it was even in his voice. There was no actual body that I saw, just his voice. I hadn't seen him in this life for four years. In the dream, I saw that we were in outer space, and there were absolutely no ties to anything. Yet, my consciousness in that moment had me changing my daughter's diaper, almost as if I was feeling the need to take care of her, even though in reality she was an adult. Behind me in a big bubble was my dad in a hospital bed asking me to come see him. I hadn't heard anything about him being ill, yet in the dream, the sensation was that he had two days to live. I found myself telling him that I had to take care of my daughter, that she had come back to live with me, and I needed to put her first.

As it happened, two days later, he died. My other sister called to tell me he had passed away, and in the meantime, I had received another call from my daughter asking me if she could come back and live with me. All this happened at the same time, and only two weeks after my mother died.

Intuition can come in all forms of consciousness.

We are not our bodies, and yet, we are creating our bodies through our belief systems, patterns, memories, etc. These forms of knowing can change your world, your life, and bring you into a better understanding of what some call "the mystery of life." A friend of mine who did healing work for a long time said, "There is no such thing as a miracle, it's just a lack of knowledge."

Just as your mind is a powerful source that we seem to feel comfortable with, so is a part of that which invents attachment. If you stop and think about it, Rumi had a quote that makes a lot of sense, especially since we are so capable of making things up. The quote is "All suffering comes from attachment." Therefore, we can identify new ways to relate to things, people, and situations just by shifting to a different perspective. Just as we can have a change in our entire being in a quantum second, we can also recognize the use of placebo.

Placebo has a definition, according to *Psychology Magazine*, Nov. 2018, that states, "The placebo effect is defined as a phenomenon in which some people experience a benefit after the administration of an active substance or sham treatment. A placebo is a substance with no known medical effects, such as sterile water, saline solution or a sugar pill." So where is this effect coming from? If it says that it is defined as a phenomenon, then how can that explain a benefit?

Our mind is creating an outcome by believing in an effect. So where is the cause coming from? There has to be a cause to create an effect. The suggestion would be that we somehow had a desire for an effect and created it. The mind doesn't know the difference. Just as there is a placebo effect, there is definitely a nocebo effect, and that is based on telling yourself the same story over and over and not creating any results.

CHAPTER FOUR

~ THE POWER OF WORDS ~

"Whatever words we utter should be chosen with care, for people will hear them and be influenced by them for good or ill." - Buddha

The English language is very interesting to me. I understand it is a very difficult language to learn for people not from an English-speaking place, and I can see why. Words like "there" have several different spellings with several different meanings, and words like "lie, tear, to, or bow" (to name only a few) have the same spellings and sometimes sounds, but different meanings, etc.

If you ask any mother trying to homeschool her child, she might say teaching English is just as challenging as raising the kid!

So why is this important in the scheme of things? Words cannot only be confusing, but their interpretations come from how we are taught. It is troublesome to *think* that a word means something that you are used to, then find in a conversation the other party is meaning something totally different with their usage. Therefore, we have many mis-interpretations and get too caught up in words.

When I lived in Hilo, Hawaii in 2006, I had the opportunity to be an "ala-kai" to Papa K Kepalino on the Big Island. I was his student and chosen as his equal for the learning of his style of Lomi Lomi massage, but also the way of aloha in working with the body. It was a good time. I am so glad that I had that time with him. Being 5th generation Kamehameha, he was noted for being a king by other kumu's (teachers) at that time.

In my first book, *The Sacred Language of the Human Body*, I noted my deep, heartfelt experience with Pele, the Volcano goddess of the aina (Island). Papa had told me a lot about the history of Hawaii and how Pele was the protector. I loved it. Then I was asked by Papa and his wife to help them out for a conference which had many Hawaiian Kupuna, elders of the Hawaiian way of healing, coming to speak in Hilo. One of those elders was Kumu John Lake. He was the sweetest, most adorable teacher at the University of Hawaii and taught Hawaiian language. To me, he looked like a Hawaiian Dick Van Dyke. You could not enter his classroom by speaking English! Only Hawaiian dialect was allowed.

I truly respected this man. He was a master of the most beautiful Hawaiian chanting songs you've ever heard. The first time he sang at the conference, he stole my heart into the land of enchantment. Every tone, every word that was sung from the heart had me in tears! I didn't know the language by studying it that well, but I knew the language by listening. I was completely mesmerized by the true aloha he sang. I learned from that moment that it is how we engage and listen with different ears that connects us. They say music is the one true language that is universal. I hear that as well. I tried to read the words on the paper when he blew me away, but I could not follow them. I was too caught up in the moment with the spirit of aloha running through my heart. He began to laugh when he asked me to do it, and even though I tried my best, I'd rather he do it!

Words can be tricky. You will hear people say, "I'm speechless" if something really affects them. Or "I can't believe you said that." And my favorite, "Bite your tongue!"

Sometimes they can demolish your real meaning, too. But then, do words ever *truly* explain how you feel? Can you put deep feelings into words? Or better yet, do you ever feel truly heard? Many clients of mine have told me over the years that no one seems to hear them or care about what they say. They are hurt over this and it causes self-esteem to slip away, or in some cases, not be there at all. I would say that at least 60% of my clients alone feel as though what they say to family members (mostly) doesn't seem to matter, as the family members have a certain expectation of how that person is and react to *that*, instead of truly listening.

Many counselors are dealing with teens that are going through tremendous peer pressure. Some of this is from being bullied or simply not having a friend that they can turn to, talk to, and associate themselves with. Unfortunately, we have proven ourselves to be a society of judgements and staunch thinking. Suicide is the highest it's ever been, and many are at a loss as to what they can do to help. If individuals learned and understood that they are holding the key to the power of the universe, maybe we would have more kindness and understanding toward each other rather than so much hurt. Words matter. **You** matter!

I was speaking at a conference with eight other healers who were handpicked by this organization to share their information with a large audience in Los Angeles. When it came to the part where we all had to do some sort of interactive experiment, there was one healer who caught my attention.

She started out by saying that there was a phrase in the bible about words and the effect they have in the universe quoted by Jesus. She did an example with dowsing rods. She had asked one man (a gent from New York) from the audience to come up on stage. She placed him at one end of the stage, and she walked all the way back to the other side of the building to where she could not go any further back (maybe 25 feet). She had her dowsing rods pointed at him and asked him to say, "The light within me sustains and guides me." Then she walked toward him and in a second, the dowsing rods showed that energy momentum expand right away! They immediately opened widely as she continued to walk toward him and stayed that way until she could go no further.

Next, she asked him to say, "I'm a piece of crap and no one likes me." All of our eyebrows raised at this point because it was so unlike anything any of us there would say or teach. But the results were amazing. Walking back to the wall, just as she had done the first time, pointing the rods forward, gave a completely different result. As she walked forward after he said that sentence, the dowsing rods stayed shut all the way up to three inches away from his body.

It was such a good experiment about how our words affect the field, not just around our own body, but through an endless universe! (personally, the man who was the subject had me laughing so hard after the experiment was finished when he blurted out, "Brooklyn Baby!")

There is another reason that I felt this chapter was necessary. Being the healer I am and witnessing what I have in people's lives as they stand before me, I must say that words are actually actions, and biofeedback of truthful statements can be intense. When we speak, not only do we affect the people and the energy around us, we can also affect our own internal selves. For example, negative self-talk can take a toll when you say things like, "My stupid ankle won't heal." Or, "My stomach always hurts." These are just a few examples of how people talk about their bodies. It may not seem like a big deal, but it really is. You are confirming that this is what happens to you. And whether this is from a present moment, or from memory, you consistently reaffirm the problem. Watching your words is necessary because they can literally encourage the reaction of your body. It is so important to be aware of this because each time you speak, you are confirming the issue.

Remember I spoke earlier about the "Spiritual Immune System"? Well, when we've had a hard or challenging experience with someone in our life, and we didn't release, resolve, or forgive it, chances are it stayed in the subconscious memory and then other patterns were created around that sensation of pain, hurt, or shame. When these feelings are left in the body without closure of some sort (hopefully an understanding of how you learned from that), then we are subject to things like an autoimmune dysfunction, adrenal overload, high blood pressure, and other symptoms. Remember that symptoms are from a cause. This means the symptom is an effect of a cause, which is the natural interpretation of the body. It is not that you are a victim, and certainly not something to blame anyone for - including yourself - but instead, it is a lesson to recognize that our thinking is not in a place that is best for us.

Many autoimmune dysfunctions are related to a conscious idea *somewhere* inside you that believes that you are not loved (cancer), or your life has changed and you can't control the outcome (thyroid), or life will never be the same and I miss my life as it was (Alzheimer's), or life should have done more for me, after all, I put out my whole life for this cause and didn't get back what I should have (Parkinson's).

There are also results in the body from discomfort around the way you were raised. Some people think that their mother or father were overbearing, and due to their sensitivity, they crumbled inside because they couldn't match up to what their parents' expectations were. This creates stomach issues, specifically colitis. There are so many autoimmune dysfunctions and each one has the pattern of how we react to a chronic situation. With cancer, which we are seeing much more of today, it really is important to know the mental and emotional cause before anything else, as these create the condition in the first place.

Cancer has many factors emotionally. It usually comes down to you and your attachment, no matter how great or small, to an old situation where you felt so badly, or so terribly left out, that you had internal, self-directed anger. We aren't usually aware of that, however it is something that I have noticed with the readings. Breast cancer is related to not enough self-nurturing. When we put other people before ourselves and are not paying enough attention to our own needs and desires, this can create malignant cells; in a case like this, it is an imbalance of the soul. Life is about receiving as well as giving, and most of the time, giving has become too overbearing and cells that are trying to keep the balance are simply thrown off.

Other cancers, such as colorectal, are related to problems in the immediate family going completely unresolved and usually has anger associated with it. One thing is for sure: nothing is random, and nothing ever happens by accident.

The wonderful author Anita Moorjani had a near death experience (NDE) from Hodgkin's disease in 2006. Her death experience is well known around the world now because she shares this so gracefully and gratefully. She wrote a book about it called *Dying to Be Me*. If you know her story, you know she was definitively pronounced dead. The doctors were profoundly amazed when she came back to her body, and within 72 hours after that, the tumors that had been riddled throughout her body that shut down her organs, began to disappear. She felt them leaving and her body getting back to normal.

The immune system is very important, as it wards off these cells within our body, so we must keep the immune system up. To do that we must remain balanced and calm. The words you use to describe how you are feeling can actually cause the immune system to stay on alert. If you say that you are always in pain, of course you give your body no other choice than to be fully on guard, almost to the point that healing will be that much more difficult in the long run because you set a pattern with your words, which became an action, which became a behavior.

The adrenal glands are so important and using the adrenaline our body produces needs to be seen like a bank account. They are not for everyday use the way most people have been using them. If you think of a bank account, you only use money when you feel you need to, or splurge with joy for a vacation, etc. We are always conscious to the best of our abilities when it comes to how we spend our money. If it is used for necessities you cannot afford, it runs out quickly.

By seeing it from this viewpoint, we can identify with how important it is to watch for how much you spend with your thoughts, your balance with sleep, or anything that is simply not necessary. The fight or flight response in the body can also be overused when it comes to protection. When we are young and in survival mode, we are on guard, but we still know how to play. Over the years as we get older, we keep the survival patterns, even when we don't need them, and that produces more adrenaline than necessary. That's why it really helps to let go of your past and start everyday as if it is completely new.

Fear and insecurity are the two main reasons the adrenals are overused. That is the "fight" response. Denial is another one, because that is subconscious patterns in the form of protection causing the individual to always be on guard, whether they know it or not. If we push our emotions down to avoid feeling, this is denial to the heart and the soul. This is just as strong as saying you know you'll get that cold every summer because you ALWAYS get a cold every summer. That's when the adrenals kick in and try to constantly answer your requests and keep you on your toes.

The body's natural state, homeostasis, is free flowing. When we pollute it with old formats of emotions and constant complaining, it can become so out of whack that the organs suffer and this becomes the norm. This is also what begins the autoimmune response; the immune system can't take much more.

As many of us know, in her story Anita told us that when she was on the other side, she saw her dad. His conversation with her was about how cancer is not a disease. It's a thought form and the body responded to fear. When he was finished speaking to her, he said, "Now go back and live your fearless self." That she did, and has ever since.

I am so very grateful to her for sharing her story in the world because the more we recognize this type of information and apply it to ourselves, the more we will naturally come to know the truth of our existence, and the power of our words.

Here are some quotes that I feel are good for us to contemplate anytime of the day:

"Once you become fearless, life becomes limitless."
- Unknown

"Life shrinks or expands in proportion to one's courage."
- Anais Nin

"How well you live depends a great deal on how well your adrenal glands function." - Mona Delfino

"The key to keeping your balance is to know when you've lost it." - Sally Rose

"Joy means retaining the balance in your mind."
- Mona Delfino

Balance, peace, and joy are the fruit of a successful life. It starts with recognizing your talents and finding ways to serve others by using them." - Thomas Kinkade

"We can change a reaction by making a new action."
- Mona Delfino

"Priorities must be set, while perceptions must be understood." - Mona Delfino

"Letting go of worry and presenting trust instead changes adrenal fatigue in to adrenal support."
- Mona Delfino

Quotes are great because they become "A-HA" moments and resonance kicks in to redirect your cells into a clarity, which helps in feeling deeper and wiser.

The body awakens with each cell, atom, and molecule resonating with each other. The voltages running through you on a daily basis are connected from the heart and teach the body how to interpret the moment. The power of words is essential to remember when we need to use them. Being aware of that will increase your ability to feel calmer in situations, keep you more current in listening to the moment, and will eventually help increase clarity in the mind and the brain.

Lessons From A Cell

1. Cells are constantly evolving to become more efficient in their destiny

2. Cells always live in the present moment

3. Cells commit totally to their purpose. They are always givers, and that makes receiving automatic.

4. Cells adapt to the now, and die to the old

5. No cell feels more important than another

6. Cells work together to enhance the purpose for the body

7. If cells aren't stimulated, they have rest periods at different stages of their life cycle

8. Cells need rest as much as they need stimulus

9. Cells rebuild their community through unity

10. Cells don't know how to lie

We don't have to be a scientist to appreciate the mechanisms of how the body works and functions. I feel so passionate as I find out more and more about the collation of cellular production, epigenetics, and this new genetic science that becomes unstoppable.

The understanding of the body from a shaman's viewpoint works like this:

A computer must be turned on to work, no matter how much info is stored. The signal of electricity is still available even in a resting state. We are always in a present genetic revolution. As creators, with or without understanding this knowledge, we know change occurs one step at a time. Yet, in quantum physics, change, no matter big or small, happens in a blink of an eye. Each second has the potential to change your life. The key here is *connection.* Without recognition on some level, being mental, emotional, spiritual, or physical, connection can lack in awareness, and therefore direction. That's why learning and living through awareness can create a more significant change every minute of every day.

Shaman know connection. They live by connection to everything. Our ancestors passed down wisdom through their DNA, and therefore, many people who feel they are extra sensitive (or highly intuitive) or are powerful healers, are people who, more than likely, have had this passed down somewhere in their bloodlines. It can be that your grandmother used to know when your mother was in trouble or was able to detect danger and be prepared.

I have spoken with many clients in the past who have told me that they loved their grandmothers or grandfathers because they just knew things. Some people tell me their connection to their grandparent or grandparents, was the best! They miss them terribly because it turns out that that grandparent was the only one they felt really *saw* them, and then encouraged them. What a wonderful feeling to know the power of love in your very own family. However, not everyone was born with this type of connection to family members. In challenging situations, it is those of us who are the leaders, the way-showers, and the teachers of this new age that learned challenging lessons as children. It's not that we are born to learn the "hard" way, but we are born to learn the tough lessons through a kind of "rite of passage" that is not the way others learn. These can be difficult lessons.

Once I went to nursing school with another student who had marks and scars all over his arms. I never said anything, but the thought ran through my head that he must have been traumatized at some point because it was obvious that these were not birthmarks.

One of the teachers asked us a question of the hardest trauma we ever had to face. It was to get us to comprehend some of the emotions patients were going to feel so we would stay sensitive to the environment. Well, this student spoke up. He said that as a child growing up in a poor area of Chicago, his mother raised him alone. He was very young when she took her pain out on him if he cried or fussed. She threatened him with a hot stove and when he did cry, she put his arm on a hot element. She deliberately burned him to "teach him a lesson." She also used a cigarette butt to burn little holes in his skin whenever she felt like it. This, needless to say, is why his arms were scarred. When asked by the teacher why he wanted to be a nurse, he replied, "So that I can be there for children in a burn unit and help them get through the emotional and mental pain, as well as the physical."

Someone like him stands out as a hero. He was quiet, never boastful. He didn't think of hurting others, and it is obvious that he really learned from this. His heart was genuine and he left an impression on me that will always be there.

CHAPTER FIVE
~ DNA: DESIGNING NEW ABILITIES ~

"A person's health isn't generally a reflection of genes, but how their environment is influencing them. Genes are a direct cause of less than one percent of diseases; 99% is how we respond to the world." - Dr. Bruce Lipton

I couldn't agree more with Bruce Lipton. I find it fascinating that the concepts we now believe are old science, are now what is known as "new genetics". According to the National Institute of Health, "new genetics" is based on how genes are related to our health. There are new directional research developments that are giving us updates in our science and education fields. When genetics first started, scientists didn't have the tools they have today. Now researchers can examine all the genes in a living organism - its genome. They now have the ability to do this all at once, as well as doing this for every species on Earth. Many experiments are still being used on mice, as they have found that mice have short life spans, which they can follow several generations and can be observed in a short period of time. They are mild-tempered and are small enough to handle.

Thanks to these tiny creatures, scientists have been able to detect how cancer thrives, how disease is tested, and can witness how DNA can regenerate and repair itself through high frequency cell reproduction. What they cannot figure out is how a mouse can have such long telomeres and such short life spans!

I have always been fascinated by certain tests that were done with mice, and one that I loved the most was in Deepak Chopra's book *Ageless Body, Timeless Mind.* In it he writes of a lab experiment where scientists put a group of rats in one cage, and another group in another cage. Each cage was given the same food at the same time. The experiment came when one cage of rats was handled daily for weeks, given love, cuddled, etc. The other group of rats were never touched or handled, just fed as normal. After a period of a few weeks with this happening every day, the rats were all fed poison. Interestingly enough, the cage of rats that were cuddled never reacted to the poison and they acted as if they were still eating food as normal. No side effect, no sickness, just regular behavior, whereas the other cage of rats died. It wasn't that they died from being unloved, they died because there was no energy to sustain them, therefore they succumbed to the poison directly.

When I read that story so very many years ago, I have to say that it changed my life. I realized that anything we feel can keep us healthy or directly cause an illness, a disease, a dis-order, and can even kill us.

So how is it that our emotions are this powerful? There are a few important answers to that.

I find the studies that prove that we actually hold memory in relation to emotions of our ancestors in our DNA fascinating. "New genetics" is teaching us about our very own evolution. I recently read a part in the book by Deepak Chopra called *Super Genes.* He describes something that I feel is important as we travel more into the universal expansion of the power we have within.

Chopra introduces researcher and British biologist, Rupert Sheldrake, who explains that according to his hypothesis, "organisms inherit habits from previous members of their species." Many studies were done with cattle on the subject of crossing grids. He stated that ranchers could save money if they knew that newer generations of cows subjected to crossing grids already knew *not* to cross them, and came to a standstill as soon as they approached either real or fake grids.

Another experiment suggests that Mohawk Indians who worked for generations on New York skyscrapers could walk on beams hundreds of feet in the air without any fear of falling. Was this inherited?

Recently I watched the popular show "America's Got Talent." One act of three brothers came on and said that their father had just passed, but they will continue the act they learned (and all were so talented in performing). They blew away the audience with their expertise that they made look so simple. They could hold each other up (with different positions of their hands) creating human geometric shapes. To anyone else, this would be impossible, but to them, it was a natural act with no fear of falling or hurting a member of their family.

Russian chess players have won the world championship many times over for similar reasons.

We seem to carry memories of bloodlines that were mostly through fear, tenacity, or some strong emotion. Remember I said earlier that a trauma can induce a pattern when the shock happens? This is why it's so important to get back on that horse after the fall, or drive again even though you were in a car accident, etc. If we don't change these behaviors, we will not be able to move forward and can possibly get stuck in life. The important thing that we must learn is that there *ARE* no accidents, and ponder why this could have happened to our best ability, without blaming or pointing fingers.

I have read in certain client's energy fields that in many cases, behavior is not only brought about by our own interpretations, but also by how our fathers and grandfathers related to life. For example, if the grandfather had a difficult time keeping the family safe, or food on the table, then this type of "knowing" through the emotion of fear or worry would be translated to the next generation.

As I am reading a client this way, I can absolutely see why people get stuck. Combine that with the way we are raised and voila! You have a set behavior already being established within your cells. It's a scientific fact that by the age of five, we are recognizing being back in a body and are adapting the best we can to our family, our peers, teachers, etc. This is what is cool though! We are our own soul and can learn what to do as we get older in any situation. If we believe that we are to follow our mothers or fathers in the way they think or try to teach us, then we grow up trying to be like our mothers and fathers and are not happy in many cases.

I remember not liking the fighting in the house as a child at that young age. One time I even ran away from home. As a matter of fact, I would leave the house any chance I could, even if I played by myself in the orange grove behind our home. Running away from problems wasn't the issue, but it was more like finding solace in places that "made more sense" to my fulfillment. Hiding under the seat of a school bus at five years old only worked so long before the bus driver was on to me.

Another interesting part of how energy affects us is that if you took a name of a partner, let's say through marriage, then you have adopted the entire bloodline of the name you chose, leaving behind the one you had. This could not only change your life with different challenges, perceptions, behaviors, and thought forms, but it can change you! We always have to remember that we are in charge, and not overlook that. Staying coherent within yourself is the ticket to balance, acceptance, allowance, release of judgment, and focus.

So, the question remains: are we truly a product of our genes?

My answer to that is yes *and* no. We are brought in with the make up to learn and live by these patterns, but we are individuals, first and foremost. We are not just a product of our family history, we are creators and beings making choices in how we can live. We are not to become a slave to an illness, or so buried in subconscious muck that we cannot see or change. Many people have shown us, whether it be through their music, through an illness, or through self-discovery, that we are never, ever victims to our gene pool. This is how the vibration of names comes into play.

When I was a child, I didn't realize that I knew things automatically. It didn't take anything for someone to throw a name out to me in conversation and I automatically perceived the feeling of that person through the vibration of their name, like catching a baseball in mid-flight. What was interesting is that later in life when I was reading energy for a living, I became more aware and discovered that I could read the essence of someone's life just by their name. So, if I first went to the heart, and that person was afraid to open up, I went through the back door and read the vibration of the name. That is how I came to know that we could then address that old memory and shift it into the now and create a chosen direction from the heart.

When we truly get that we are not our genes and consciously find that our environment is instigating beliefs and behaviors, we will become more aware of our abilities. Abilities are never stuck, no matter how you think of yourself. They are there; maybe from lifetimes of information not consciously connected, but they are definitely there. If you were a piano player in another life, chances are you may have a draw to pianos in this life, and so on.

I always look at past lives like a calendar. Even though we are in new bodies, many times we come back to continue what we didn't finish, or have a different purpose that we decide we want to live this time around. Most of the people I have had the opportunity to work with have started a new life to continue from an old one. By reading the lifespan on an energetic level, there is no time. However, living in one body can only go so far, and each life is a new opportunity to recreate something you were not successful with before. How we do that depends on how we open up to recognition of self-esteem and taking back our personal recognition of freedom.

Abilities are meant to be expanded, just as we need to grow from childhood to adulthood.

I recently learned an interesting fact from an article in *ScienceDaily* on epigenetics: "Epigenetics now uses chemistry to create genetic memories of past experiences, which are much more recent and intimate than the 2.8 billion-year-old memories that originally built the DNA molecule."

This means we have new studies being done, thank goodness, as well as acceptance from scientists that are willing to do this kind of research. These are not only exciting times, but clearly we are learning new concepts of evolution as creators, and now we are being engaged in it. The wisdom of our ancestors is crucial because it is a form of life that was ingrained into each of us for a reason. It doesn't mean we have to live the way they did, for that was a totally different time.

Today, it's like we are returning back to a way of life that feels good. We are eating healthier, growing the food we eat organically - we don't even mind paying a little more money at local health food stores to get what we feel is best for us. There is also a craze in working out, as we are learning that adult obesity rates have soared to 35% (as of this year) since 2010. Furthermore, adults are realizing that our stress rates are up. The percentage of that is out of this world!

STRESS LEVELS AND TELOMERES

Studies have recently shown that stress levels in adults and children are up significantly. Most Americans alone are suffering from moderate to high stress, with 44% reporting that their stress levels have definitely increased over the past five years. Fears about job stability and money issues are topping the charts, and that is causing 75% to 90% of all doctor visits to be from stress-related ailments.

The diagnoses are endless, and with autoimmune diseases on the rise, our body will continue to drop in its health if stress reduction isn't recognized first as a priority. We know eating healthy is important, however causes from stress will outweigh our poor immune system causing the adrenals to be too stressed, and for some people, this affects their digestion and high blood pressure occurs. This is only to name a few things that we seem to be seeing more and more of in our world today. As a matter of fact, the mortality due to stress-related illness is higher than doctors have ever witnessed before.

So, what about aging with stress? Can we actually bring in new abilities to change the process of the end caps of our DNA to repair themselves? Yes, we can. This takes conscious attention and a desire to reduce your stress levels. One important point that needs to be mentioned is that people who are stressed out and operating on adrenal overload, are developing illnesses at an alarming rate. Cancer, thyroid, blood pressure, and diabetes, are just a few diagnoses on the upswing. In the energetic world, these have different reasons but the same results: they become autoimmune dysfunctions.

Every diagnosis has a specific cause:

Cancer: The true energy source that drives us to get cancer is self-directed anger on some level because we take on doing too much, such as working too hard or too long. Paying attention to the heart and the feelings of emotions around anger, sadness, feeling abused, etc. can stress out the adrenal glands, making the immune system weak. This isn't to say that everyone who works too hard or constantly stays in a state of emotional overwhelm gets cancer. It is, however, saying that there is an underlying cause related to why cell mutation and growth occur. There are many forms of cancer, and many places cancer can show up. Even though the doctors have their place for acknowledging it and helping us through it via conventional means, again, we must look deeper within ourselves to see the related cause. Many people who have had cancer and lived through it will tell you that it was an eye-opener. It was, in a strange and confrontational way, a blessing. It's a very tough challenge to go through, however this is where you find what really matters in life, how many people you wanted to say I'm sorry to, and mostly, it makes you recognize how to take better care of yourself on every level. Emotional causes will have a stare down with you. You're now at your most vulnerable moment. As Anita Moorjani has mentioned to us, fear can be the culprit underneath all the ways we try to avoid it. You learn that stress took its toll, and hopefully will make sure you take more vacations, go to bed on time by listening to the body, and feed yourself with healthy foods. You live more aware. Your immune system needs your love.

The lesson of cancer is to do all the things you want and explore the giving, the forgiving, and the receiving that life has to offer. Stress comes in holding on to subconscious ideas around avoidance (fear), working too hard, or feeling unloved.

Thyroid: I mentioned thyroid in my last book, *The Sacred Language of the Human Body*, as a control issue. *Hypo*thyroid is not feeling good enough, or enough to get over that hump. Self-esteem is unrecognizable for the most part, while *hyper*thyroid is insecurity too, but this is deciding that you must be in control. This master gland does not know how to balance when the psyche is determined to believe a certain way. Stress comes in trying too hard to protect or simply be in control.

Blood Pressure: Your BP is an indicator of what you are perceiving. If you are under pressure somehow, this is how the heart tries to keep you where you want to be, until you feel thrown off. Systolic (the high number) of the BP is what is going on outside of you. How much pressure you feel is happening that you may feel responsible for (stress)? Diastolic (low number) is what is happening inside you. How do you really feel? Are you doing what your heart tells you? What excuses are you using to prevent balance? BP is critical for understanding because it is directly related to your heart and actions through the emotional body. Stress comes in not listening to a part of you and your needs.

Diabetes: Any autoimmune dysfunction is an eye opener. Since diabetes is on the rise and millions of Americans are at risk for type 2 diabetes, this is an indicator that stress hits hard here, and the way we view life is crucial to our health in any situation. With diabetes, the energetic cause suggests that we have lost the "sweetness of life." Dr. Paul Robertson from the journal of *Biological Chemistry* says that "diabetes is caused by chronic oxidative stress (a condition in which there is an imbalance between antioxidants and free radicals in the body) as a central mechanism for glucose toxicity in pancreatic islet beta cells" (Insulin producing cells). An imbalance is a struggle in the body. If someone feels trapped by a partner or maybe a parent, and doesn't feel their worth is taken into account on a large scale, someone could possibly get an onset of diabetes, no matter what age.

Parkinson's Disease: In Parkinson's, it's a chronic disease that is slow moving because nerves are dying due to a lack of messaging from dopamine (a neurotransmitter) activity in the brain to the body, therefore causing lack of movement in the body. Doctors do not know exactly how Parkinson's happens, however, in energy work, I have discovered that the mental cause is a form of believing that you put your whole life toward something and felt it was important, but your peers did not either appreciate it or you found that you didn't get back as much as you put out. Therefore, it becomes a case where the brain begins to shut down where dopamine is generated, and being a neuro-hormone, flexibility in muscle movement depends on dopamine. Walking, eating, thinking, etc. reacts to this, which makes the body movements much slower and more difficult.

Stress related mental and emotional concepts have invaded the body so the body actually has little or no defense to it. Stresses like these can cause aging to occur faster and leave us feeling tired without the energy we need to think clearly, breathe deeply, and go about our day without feeling drained.

Telomeres are the caps that end the DNA strand, however, they fray, just like the split end of a hair. When all the stresses continue to keep us in a fight-or-flight response, we will age early. If, on the other hand, you meet people who are in their 70's and are youthful, playful, open-hearted, and still have that sense of humor, you may be amazed that they can be at that age and look so young! Age is a number. This still baffles the medical community though, because they haven't witnessed the internal behavior of patients, only their age in these cases.

I can tell you after many years of loving this energy work I do with individuals, we are capable of changing all of it beyond our wildest dreams... at any minute! Every single choice you make modifies and changes the activity of each cell. This is the beauty of quantum energy. Living in the moment is the ticket to living. When we combine our mental, emotional, and spiritual essence to align with the soul, we feel good. You recognize balance and find yourself motivated to enjoy every moment after another. That's why age can take a back seat, unless you let it be the driver. Choices continuously remain to be our existence. This is also known as free will.

When I hear that term, I feel so empowered. I loved the movie with Jim Carrey called "Bruce Almighty". So many parts in that movie had me laughing non-stop! When Morgan Freeman (who plays God) tells Jim Carrey (playing Bruce) it's ok if he takes the role for a week, Bruce is shocked; then he gets cocky and everyone is winning the lottery! One thing God tells Bruce is there are two things you do not want during this time. 1) Don't mess with free will, and 2) Don't tell anyone because you don't want that kind of attention!

Of course, in the movie, he tries to mess with the free will of his girlfriend, and everything falls apart. Such a good lesson for us to remember that *everyone* has lessons. When we remember to live our lives the best we can without all that self judgement, and without trying to interfere in other people's lives, we can be much more compassionate to others, especially people who are close to us.

Lessons are the reason we come back. We are here to discover the power we have within to create and manifest better lives on every level. Knowing that the body is a receiver, and you are the antenna to be able to broadcast who you are, is a magnificent discovery. We are all on the same roller coaster, just in different cars. Some people throw their arms in the air and say, "Let's do this", when others clutch the bar so tight as to be riding in resistance all the way. Resistance will have its consequences, and resilience in a world of change will allow you to have spontaneous joy and new creation. You are the "new genetics" in action!

CHAPTER SIX
~ BEING ENGAGED IN THE SELF ~

When I first thought about writing this book, I kept having moments where I felt these "downloads" (messages from spirit) coming in so I could share with you the excitement I feel, like when I have a student who is ready to take off and run with the information.

These downloads are spontaneous in the moment, no matter what I'm doing. Sometimes they can come at 3:00am with new information. I have recently heard other people tell me that they have also been waking up at different times of the night with emotions, possibly brought on by dreams.

The times we are in are like a collective diamond in the rough. Our days are busy and time for ourselves seems to never be enough. However, when these expressions of the soul come through, no matter what, when, how or where, that is a connection. Those are shining moments from within that hit the psyche and cause us to ponder. Pondering is not wondering. Pondering is, according to the dictionary, "Thinking about something carefully, especially before making a decision, or even reaching a conclusion." Wondering is more of a desire to know something, or very curious.

So, what are these downloads about? Mine have been happening on a regular basis. Even before I decided to write the book, information was pouring in, like a waterfall over the top of my head, asking for me to pay attention to these ideas - these wise, connected, quiet conversations -

until I had to write them down. I thought they were for articles, and some were, but when your whole life is being run by deep intuitive awareness, it's time to move mountains. What are some of the ways we can become better engaged within ourselves, or better yet, connected or aligned to the self?

Here are a few techniques you can use to increase your awareness and self-connection, and these can help you become more deeply aware without thinking so much. Self-awareness takes time and practice.

1. Keep a journal. Writing can entice a form of biofeedback and create a wholeness within. This gives you more flexibility, more insights, and more contemplation of yourself.

2. Find a way to perform daily self-reflection. Listen to your words and allow interpretations to shift with new perceptions. Growth is expansion.

3. Take a personality test. You can go online these days and check these out. Then you can see what else you can learn about yourself that can entice motivation for your soul!

4. Practice meditation or mindfulness. Any form of being more aware of your actions will shift the reactions. As above, so below. As within, so without.

There's no doubt that meditation calms the energetic field and connects you to your higher self. Many people find that meditation is not for them, so yoga is the next best thing to keep you in a state of balance. Remember, in a quantum universe, it only takes a second for a connection to take place. It can take up to a minute to have an "A-HA" moment that changes your life, or a minute to think a thought that your life is in ruins. Five minutes of true, quiet stillness is as important as a year of self-help classes!

5. Write down future goals. When we have motivation behind an action, it's like getting on a surfboard and hoping the wave will take us for a fun ride! What actually gets that momentum going is being ready and willing for a change that inspires you. We want to stay open to possibilities.

6. Ask for feedback from trusted friends or partners, or even from co-workers. As tough as that might be, or challenging to hear constructive criticism, find a time that feels right. Maybe take a friend out to dinner, or coffee. These moments are precious and can be harder on the person you're asking than on you. So, keep open, write things down if you need to, but remember this is constructive. You'll grow from the experience.

7. Pause between activities and consider how you are feeling. This is your ticket to contemplation of your true self. In this place, we can feel a calling, or a nudge as to which way to sway. After I have coffee with a friend, or spend time at a meeting, I walk away with a new outlook. Remember, these aren't necessarily good or bad, they're just the motivation to discover more about what floats your boat.

8. Listen and receive. How many times have you felt that the past haunted you, or still does, with how much you are *supposed* to give and do for others? Giving is great, up until you give out because you don't have the fuel to resource your actions. We get tired. We drop our energy level because there is not enough nurturing for us left in our bag of adrenals. Even if you just take a hot bath, go outside and look at the stars, or take a few moments to laugh at a joke; small things create big ice breakers. Listening teaches us to unite ourselves to more engagement. Receiving feeds the heart.

9. Engage with conversation, activities, or what helps you with more passion. This is like receiving, but mostly it's where I spoke of "stretching ourselves" to say yes to an activity that normally we would say no to.

10. Pay attention to life! Remember the movie, "Michael" with John Travolta? I loved when Andi McDowell's role as an "angel expert" was confronted by Michael when he wanted her to join the group and go to Chicago. When she declined, he went to her and said, "You will go to Chicago or I'll have to tell everyone that you aren't an angel expert." Stunned, she asked him, "How do you know?" His response was, "I pay attention." Life will open doors in ways that will make you drop your jaw if you become aware of your place in the moment. Let's say a butterfly flies right in front of you, or a dragonfly, or a hummingbird. You are surprised - they caught you off guard. What is your first reaction? Hopefully it's a happy moment! When you combine the totem meaning with what you were doing or thinking seconds before, you will get a confirmation; the happy surprise was not an accident.

Butterfly is transformation. Dragonfly is illumination from illusion, and hummingbird is joy. This is an example that there is a much larger picture going on here.

One story I have is when my soulmate dog passed away in 2016. Kita was the best: a Siberian Husky who saved my life twice. The day I had to put her down from cancer is the day that I was moving from one house to another. I had her for nine years. I used to laugh when I played YouTube videos she loved of Mishka, the talking husky. When I played those videos, she howled exactly like Mishka did. And when Mishka's owner said, "I love you", Mishka responded with words that sounded very much like "I love you"! So, I taught Kita how to say I love you… and every time, she did it! Then one day I noticed that Mishka was limping in one of the videos and the owner was so torn up. He just found out that Mishka had cancer on the shoulder of her left leg.

These cancers in dogs are difficult, to say the least, and Mishka didn't make it. I still played the videos for Kita, but it was almost like Kita knew Mishka wasn't really there. It was about three months later my girl got cancer herself and passed away, no matter what I did to try to stop it. Being the healer I am, I did **everything** I knew how, and realized this was her choice. She was done.

And with that, so were the lessons I learned with her. Now it was time for me to move on too. What happened was miraculous, as she knew where to lay down in the backyard. I was singing a ceremony song for her that I sang many times before with her there with me. This time it was for her. As I sang and the vet was in the backyard with us, I felt something on my cheek. I stopped singing and opened my eyes for a moment, and on my left cheek was a huge yellow butterfly. It just sat there, like it was giving me a kiss. I was shocked, then I looked at the vet, and my Kita, and then I saw that Kita had gone to sleep and the vet had dropped her jaw. She told me she had never seen anything like that before, and she *KNEW* it was Kita's spirit. The butterfly went from my cheek to my shoulder as I sobbed, and didn't leave until I took a breath. From that moment on, I have not seen a butterfly that size, nor that special. Other pretty ones, yes, but this one was the connection that will live in my heart forever.

Being engaged is a form of connection that says you know that something matters. It's not what happens to you, it's how you accept something. It isn't even attachment. A healthy attachment is a bond between a mother and child, for instance, or it can happen in relationships. The difference between attachment and engaging is that engaging comes from the heart. It's you being you in the moment.

Attachment happens when you hook in with someone or something, however the vibe is not always healthy. When Rumi said, "The root of all suffering comes from attachment", I believe he meant that letting go is difficult, and therefore we can find ourselves unsure as to how to become independent of someone else's decisions, thoughts, or even bad habits.

Engaging in conversation is a form of being present. When we engage in a project, we put our heart into it without needing someone else's opinion, and we feel good about recognizing our own intentions and doing something about it. Engagement and attachment are two different things.

One download I received that I'll share was about connection to the self. I was being shown how important everything that happens to us is, showing us that with every action is a reaction. How we feel and respond to everything we touch, everyone we meet, every moment we are doing our job or raising our family, this is all a form of biofeedback. Giving and receiving is interaction, yet it is teaching us about the self.

Are we learning new things about how we used to feel when we react? When you hear yourself saying or acting out like you used to, and realizing it doesn't suit you anymore, this is actually connecting to the self. Some call it the dance of life.

Looking back on certain relationships or conversations, or even how you felt about someone, is biofeedback to your heart. It doesn't really matter if you consider it good or not. It is the lesson of how we accept or accepted this. Was it their fault the relationship didn't work? Were we too sensitive? Either way, it was how we engaged in it, or not. Taking those lessons and learning from them is difficult when we are personally affected emotionally. We are such creatures of habit from familiarity. (Isn't it interesting how the word "familiarity" seems to be a derivative of the word "family?")

There are several analogies that can be mentioned to help see the truth. For example, as I've mentioned earlier, life is like a bank account. In reference to engaging in the self, you must recognize that how much you have put out is just as important as how much you get back. If we didn't make money, our account would be empty, so we need to receive money to fill the bank account. If you put your attention to helping people too much, you are depleting the account by not receiving as much. Some will say they get fed by helping. I am the first one to admit that I felt that way for years. If someone asked me, "How do you keep working like this?" I'd always say, "There's more where that came from!" I was so happy to feel that way. Then I was faced with an illness that held me accountable for that idea, resulting in me having to rest for a few months. I learned from experience that it truly is all about balance!

Bringing back energy for yourself is crucial for your sanity, your stamina, and your life. People who have partners will sometimes be submissive as to keep the peace. However, that needs some examining in order to make it a more fulfilling and happy relationship for both people. Letting the spiritual bank account go empty doesn't give you freedom. Debt can be emotional as well as mental. One way to feed yourself in any situation is to say out loud that you are awesome! It is not easy for people to do this, and if we expect others to, we may be sorely disappointed.

THE BIG BANG

Let's say you are engaging in a conversation with a friend, and the friend brings up something that reminds you of a good time that you both shared together. That memory is a thing. It's like a big bang effect because the two of you shared in something that triggered the same response. What that does is unite two thoughts, two memories, and then it becomes a whole; the two become one, increasing and confirming a shared energy. The magnitude of the relationship that was just confirmed in that dialogue created the memory all over again and the hearts engaged in a oneness. This is the "two or more are gathered" effect. The concept around this type of connection brought a joyful experience back to the present moment, and therefore, time was obsolete. This is the meaning of consciousness.

Doing this as an individual is similar, however the engagement becomes connection to your mind and your heart.

Thinking is so constant that we rarely give ourselves a break from it. But how much of that thinking is mindless? How much is mindful? Inner chatter can become like the "monkey mind" all over the place. The "monkey mind" is a Buddhist term that indicates being unsettled, restless, or confused.

I remember an episode of the popular TV sitcom "The Big Bang Theory." Sheldon Cooper is a nerdy scientist who is extremely annoying to his friends and co-workers. He talks constantly about anything that comes to his mind. Fortunately, the show made him funny! In one episode, he gets a bit quiet at their lunch table, so Howard, his friend says, "Sheldon, what's wrong?" Sheldon responds, "Nothing, I'm just thinking about a book I read." Now I'm thinking about my lunch. Now I'm thinking about trains. I love trains." I guess you could say he was trying to have "a train of thought". (pun intended!)

While our minds are busy trying to conform to what might be happening around us, how much of this is considered important? Being in the moment doesn't require thought. It's observation. Observation is recognition. These are quiet concepts that can fill our awareness just as much as thought, but even more. The moment keeps you balanced. This then becomes engaging. You cannot necessarily be engaged by thinking. It has to be deeper, in your own awareness, that your consciousness reveals answers to questions you never asked. Consciousness *is* connection. It is a sense of focus, yet taking in several things at once without feeling that your mind is being overloaded.

When someone is conscious, they automatically have memory because they are engaged in the moment. I learned this many years ago when I became cognizant of being in my body at 6 months old. I can remember it like it was yesterday because there was no time, only experience.

When people get headaches or migraines, the energetic cause behind that is confusion. What decision do I (or should I) make? Headaches are not making a choice and migraines are knowing what choice to make but not making it. Vertigo is another condition people get in relation to feeling overwhelmed with the same patterns they have been living without realizing it consciously. This can be related to ringing in the ears. Tinnitus is yet another form of your body trying to get your attention. That biofeedback is definitely working!

BREAKING BARRIERS

Many people want to know their past lives; what they did and who they were. I'll fill you in on a little secret. You are still similar to what lives you've lived because all that information from other lifetimes is still within you. That's why sometimes there is a feeling we get of "unfinished business". Or we meet someone and swear we met them before. But it isn't that past lives dictate what you are today, it is just that at that time, you chose to make some form of decision through the situations you were faced with.

If you were a combat soldier, (which **many** people who have come back are), you may feel very sensitive to your actions and not want to hurt anyone in this lifetime. This could end up being a detriment to you this time around. To be over-sensitive to others is denying your true self, and it can be like a chameleon changing colors for different environments. What we don't realize is that chameleons do that to avoid danger. So, is it out of insecurity that we try to react this for others? I would say yes, and have witnessed it several times in many clients.

It's a subconscious concept realizing we came back to possibly "make amends" for what we did the last time. Yet we never lost our beautiful heart. Can you imagine being a soldier and having to kill others in war, knowing that that person had a family and was similar to you? When we cross over, we see this. We feel this and are confronted with it. When we come back, we will automatically react to any situation that triggers this cause.

If we are children and get yelled at, we may cry wondering what we did "wrong". By not pleasing our parents, are we in fear? These are called "carry-overs" from other lifetimes. Until we make new decisions (and that is what happens to us when we are five, six and seven years old), we won't know *how* to be who we are until we see that insecurities are the culprit for not giving yourself respect, approval, or permission to be ok just being you.

When we get older, we are faced with choices that will either keep us committed to patterns we know are *not* who we are, or we need to break the cycle. Sometimes that requires a very uncomfortable situation of standing up for yourself. Whatever method you use, be kind to yourself. People only go as far as they feel comfortable with, and they need to be ready. If you are in between and **know** that change needs to be done and you don't do so, you can end up with inner anxiety and nervous reactions.

The teeth are memories from past lives as well. Bones, nails, hair, and teeth are all about past life memories. With your teeth, the nerves in the mouth are affected when a triggered response from something coming up from your past appears.

When I help people release these very old traumas, sure, we can go into the cause by witnessing the effect. Also, we can uncover other reactions in the body when we were actually working on something else.

For example, I had a man I worked on who called to get help for headaches. What we discovered was that he had hypertension and was ready for a heart attack. Remembering that everything is energy, I asked him questions to engage him with me in this healing. He agreed that he wasn't breathing to his full capacity and noticed a few chest pains that came and went. When we got to the heart, I asked him questions about his wife and his relationship that I felt was coming from him.

The truth was he was having an affair and didn't want to tell me. But this affected him so much that no matter how he tried to deny it, he was blaming himself subconsciously and it was killing him. Of course, I had to bring it up and suggest that he may want to "make a decision" for himself. Either stop the affair, change his life, or forgive himself. I told him this was not about whether I cared or not about *his* choice, because healing work has no judgment at all. He mentioned he loved the other lady and had been with her for a while but didn't want to leave his wife. When I asked him why, he said he would lose everything. This was causing pressure to build and there was "no way out" for his situation, in his mind. He was ready to explode. However, once we connected to the information from the heart, he later made a choice and figured it out.

I had another client who didn't want to hurt her dad, and so ended up being his caretaker. I have actually had many clients in this predicament. Whether it be their mothers or fathers, by being their caregiver in the end, it can cause more stress than necessary. The client feels committed to be the one to take care of their ailing parents, so they do. Yet the memory of how they were raised is front and center the whole time, and in the background, the subconscious memories are reminding them about how their lives became what they did; some are highly resentful. I hear them tell me, "He's impossible. My dad has always been impossible to deal with." Or, "My mother doesn't listen to me. She really never did," and so on.

When someone asks me how to deal with these stresses, I must look at this from their "soul contract" and let them know the energy of it. Usually it is to make peace with the parent before they cross over. One way you do that is to make peace with yourself first and realize you changed over all these years, and no matter how difficult it is emotionally in these situations, there's also a healing being suggested as an opportunity. Here is where attachment must be recognized, and this is where you engage in yourself by seeing that A) this won't last forever, and B) you are learning a lot about your feelings toward your past in order to change them.

As Michael Jackson's hit song, "Man in the Mirror" says:

"I'm gonna make a change, for once in my life.
It's gonna feel real good, gonna make a difference,
Gonna make it right."

I wouldn't say you're "making it right", but instead, you are connecting to your inner self, aligning with your truth, and making a choice to be who you really are. This is wisdom. To be able to understand that you can create your life from the inside out means that you can create a significant change to anything you put your mind to.

I remember talking to my Cherokee mentor one time several years ago about how I was raising my kids, how my job seemed overwhelming, etc. She took one look at me and said, "You did nothing wrong, Mona." That stopped me in my tracks from every possible negative thought that could have initiated after that! I did nothing wrong. What a concept. As I pondered that "A-HA" moment, I found myself asking her, "Then what do I do from here?" She smiled at me and simply said, "Enjoy."

This is how I have lived my life since; still learning, still laughing at myself, and the most important thing I learned was to stop with negative self-talk, judgement of any kind, and to read why and how people live their lives.

When we accept this, it can turn our lives around. In truth, the power inside you is unstoppable.

CHAPTER SEVEN
~ THE POWER OF SUGGESTION ~

That unstoppable power is what keeps us moving, growing, changing, and adapting. Those 7 trillion volts constantly running through our bodies are always on the lookout for the next adventure, whether contemplating our next meal, deciding what we will do in an hour, or planning our week.

The power of suggestion is so real that your life can change in a minute if someone says something to you and you instantly hear what they say through an emotional response. What happens when a co-worker comes to you and says, "The boss is really mad at you and says you didn't meet the deadline for that project last year." Compare that to the same person coming up to you and saying, "The boss said you did an amazing job on the project you did last week." The difference is remarkable. The receptors in your body get all giddy with delight with the second statement. The first statement sends you into panic, fear, disgrace, failure, etc. After all, it feels almost like a death sentence for your job, your future jobs, your relationships, and so on. The trick here is to see how easily flustered we get when we are confronted with something uncomfortable.

When a doctor tells you that he will have to take blood and you are afraid of needles, you first shake in your seat, then you may start sweating, all before you even get to the lab. At the lab you may find yourself closing your eyes with a scrunched-up face in fear over the initial contact of the needle. Some people can feel the needle even if it isn't touching them. These kinds of experiences happen all the time. Memory comes with expectation, and that is deeply subconscious. We can create the pain even before it occurs.

However, we can also stop pain before it happens.

Tibetan Buddhist monks practice an advanced meditation technique called "tumo". They intentionally look at the palm of their hand until it gets red; then they feel the warmth. As it gets warmer, it gets even more red. They use this technique to warm their whole body, and they sit in freezing ice caves overnight wearing nothing but a saffron robe. If someone practices this effect repeatedly, they can train their bodies to always be regulated and not affected by the cold whatsoever.

The traumas we encounter are stuck in the subconscious, and the mind automatically regulates the next response. We need to realize that the mind is trying to protect us through old experiences and will respond with an emotional reflex. However, we are capable of changing that as well.

A client of mine several years ago came to see me. She walked in as a new client and told me that she was going to commit suicide. I looked at her and said, "Why would you want to do that when you are so pretty and such a sweet person?" She bluntly said, "My husband left me for another woman." A look must have come over my face that caught her attention. I remarked, "You want to kill yourself over a man? Especially one like that?" She became totally silent and made a small noise, as if she got it. Then she said, "Well when you put it like that, it does sound silly doesn't it?" We both laughed it off and the healing began.

The power of suggestion often happens when we aren't expecting it. We go about living our lives, and while walking through a grocery store, can overhear someone talking. That may initiate us to pay attention even if we aren't really listening. Jesus said, "In my Father's house there are many mansions." It truly is the amount of biofeedback, recognitions, and even subconscious attractions that get our attention. Again, it's not good or bad. It just is. All and everything is a teacher. "When the student is ready, the teacher appears" is a popular quote from Buddha. On some level, we are all ready for the *next adventure.*

The power of suggestion can spark an "A-HA" moment as well, depending how receptive we are. One simple suggestion can make or break us. If someone hands you a sugar pill and says that it's headache medicine and you'll feel better in no time, you have that in mind if you take it. Most certainly you will be better "in no time." This is an energy exchange. Our bodies are constantly being affected even without having to "think."

Bruce Lipton's first book is called *The Biology of Belief.* I encourage anyone to read it, keeping in mind the placebo and nocebo effects. We are always acting and reacting on environmental influences, whether they be from the past or current. Will they always affect our future? Yes, unless we become resilient enough to confront a situation and change it.

When I do energy work with clients, most of the time there has been a trauma, which keeps inspiring another trauma until that energy changes and shifts. Once recognized, that client will move on, unless they have a desire not to, and that is the choice they are making. However, in these positive changes for growth, self-awareness, and motivation, *this* is what makes us co-creators, cultural creators, and leaders. Anyone who has had abuse, been bullied, or had negative experiences sometimes will fall into the same behavior pattern as their abuser because they never understood the difference, only the trauma. This is where we keep in mind that attachment falls into this category. The more we learn that the heart can make these changes, the more we live up to our own courageous abilities.

PLACEBO AND NOCEBO

Placebo is the positive response to any treatment or suggestion without an active substance intervening. It's amazing the power of the mind... all through acceptance. There have been several studies of the placebo effect that help with enthusiasm, good communication, listening skills, and even increasing self-reputations. That is how powerful our mind is.

When we are uptight through stress, or patterns that have a strong hold on us (fear is a big culprit), this in turn affects the cortisol level, which in turn affects the adrenal glands, which in turn affects our sleep patterns, digestion, brings on depression, premature aging, high blood pressure, mood swings, etc. Yet, if we are around loving people, nurturing our senses, believing in ourselves, this can change. "Love is the answer" means ALL is well, and illnesses can become strengths.

There was a winning act on the TV show *America's Got Talent* where an 11-year-old boy was bullied in school. When Simon, one of the judges who designed the show itself, asked him why he had been bullied, he told Simon (and 4,000 other people in the audience) that he had cancer and kids made fun of him. He was only four years old when he was diagnosed with leukemia. He had only been in remission for four years when he was on the stage. He felt music would help his frustration. He took up the violin and became so good that he got into competitions, etc. He was so good in fact, that he won the ultimate "golden buzzer" award and would go through to the end of the competition.

Music is one of the most inspiring antidotes for pain, frustration, a buildup of anger, etc. It automatically soothes the nerves and can actually change the environmental field. Classical music has had the ability to change brainwaves. Playing an instrument has created more brain power for sparking the electromagnetic field into more peace and satisfaction. Playing music for babies before they are born (and after) creates a sensory-engaging environment that contributes to the child's cognitive and sensory development.

Mozart and Bach's music specifically has an emotional and psychological healing effect on people in the hospital as well. It definitely helps with healing after surgery. If doctors played that for patients, they would see much more results and shorter stays in recovery.

There is also something called the "nocebo effect", which is just as important to understand as the "placebo effect". Nocebo was studied at Harvard Medical School, and it was found that when a patient was given a sugar pill and told that this pill had terrible side effects, the patient began to experience the side effects given by the suggestion of the doctor who was prescribing it. Here is the power of suggestion at work.

Dr. John Kelly, Ph.D., the deputy director at Harvard, mentions that it's surprising how similarly the side-effect profile for the placebo often mirrors the side-effect of the active treatment. He says it's the power of the imagination. "If you ask someone to imagine a visual scene in their minds, you can see on an MRI that their occipital lobes, the part of the brain involved with vision, are activated. If you tell someone to imagine doing some physical activity, you will see the motor cortex showing activation. Just imagining something happening is enough to activate those portions of the brain associated with that, or worry, or pain."

I have seen this for myself several times with people, but one interesting time was when I was nursing. The doctor I had worked with was quick and very witty. We had a patient who kept coming in with migraines. One day when he came in for his checkup, the doctor got a bit flustered when he realized that we were out of the medication we normally gave him as an injection. We had nothing else at the immediate time to give him, so the doctor suggested that we give him a shot of water. I looked at him rather funny, and then he said that he believed this would help him, and after the injection we would keep him in the room for observation. We did, and lo and behold, he said he was fine and asked to leave. I was stunned as I was watching placebo in action 40 years ago and smiled knowing it was "all in his head".

Dr. Kelly also mentioned that, "Believing in placebo doesn't necessarily reduce brain tumors or heal broken bones. But it can work with subjective outcomes, like the degree to which you feel pain, or nausea, or even depression."

In energy medicine, this can be extended further. I understand his analysis, yet I have witnessed many wonderful outcomes due to the power of the mind, the imagination, and mostly the desire in a person who wants to heal.

One thing we can agree on is that we should think positively about the medicine and treatments we receive and believe that the benefits will far outweigh the risks. If you can do that, you will increase your chances of having a good outcome.

TALKING TO THE SELF

Since the power of suggestion is our theme here, then what about self-talk? This is a doozy! Every part of the body has its own consciousness. The heart has brain cells and the brain actually has heart cells. You are capable of thinking with the heart and feeling with the brain. The body has its own memory, storage unit, and acts like a radio. They are receptors and transmitters. These cells, including stem cells, are major players in your life. They are always in alignment to your thoughts, but even more interesting, they are your indicators when there is something out of alignment to the point where they must break down, or multiply out of control, to show you.

When you talk to your body, you are not just the captain at the control tower. You are actually engaging in teamwork and telling the worker bees what the queen wants. Analogies are great! They help us to really comprehend an action, and in this case, present direction, like a coach for a baseball team. Remember I discussed the part about where two or more are gathered? Connection is the key to consciousness, therefore, spending time connecting with your body and talking to it can literally have your team listening, and winning the game!

The body also likes cycles. It can operate on a daily basis with the same intention. For example, many years ago, I had a daycare when my children were very little. It was a success, as the kids were amazing, creative, and obedient for nap time.

One day I had a little girl come into the daycare who was about three years old. She had never been to a daycare before, and following direction was very difficult for her. She didn't seem to understand nap time. This would have to change soon, for daycare mommy needed her breaks too! When one o'clock came and it was time to put the little rascals to rest, she cried hysterically, working herself into a tizzy. I laid down with her and sang to her, told her stories, until she felt comfortable enough with me to quiet down. The second day she was with us, she got more comfortable with the other children. As she watched their behavior, she started to adapt. By the third day, she fell asleep right at one o'clock, and by the fourth day, she couldn't keep her eyes open.

I learned that children respond and adapt to their environment, and in 24 to 36 hours, it was already pretty much a done deal. What was funny was that her parents worked a lot, and so on the weekends they wanted to go play and do things with their little girl. The first weekend they had together after her first week in my daycare, the mom told me they were on a hike, and right at one o'clock her daughter laid down in a nearby grassy area and fell asleep. No matter what they did, they couldn't keep her awake, so back to the truck they went. On Sunday, they tried it again, and the same thing happened.

At first, they were a bit upset wondering why this was happening, and then I explained that all the children rested for about an hour at one o'clock, and their little girl did too. Astonished, they said she had never napped. Not even when she was a year old. She had ADD. (Attention Deficit Disorder) and had no real direction or boundaries; yet now she did. The other children were her helpers, due to the environment.

What this tells us is that the body also interprets cycles. It remembers what happened when you were in that car accident and got whiplash. To break any pattern, you have to connect, talk to, or recognize the situation, and instead of saying out loud, "My stupid neck will never heal from that whiplash", or, "I broke my arm and it will never be the same", etc., we must remember the body listens. By engaging in your senses, you can identify with what emotion the pain has.

Sharp pain is from acute trauma. Dull pain is more related to chronic pain or long-standing difficulties in any situation that hasn't been released. Bruising is sensitivity and possibly feeling hurt by someone else. Sudden pain, depending on where it is, is you and your body getting your attention. For example, stubbing your toe or hitting your funny bone on the corner of a table.

These kinds of pains are not accidents. They are an initial connection to help you wake up to something else that is subconsciously bothering you. Toes are indicative of moving forward, but also how are you feeling about that new job? Do you have doubts that you will be good enough? Elbows are the flexibility (or lack thereof) in what you are carrying.

This goes on and on in the body, which is why it is important to have proper self-talk to the self and your body as you are becoming higher in your consciousness, more aligned to the true soul, and finding that self-directed freedom we are all looking for.

Here are a few key steps of how you can help to communicate with the body (*These guidelines are quoted by Therese Wade, with the site ConsciousReminder.com, who had a successful experience with her body after surgery*):

1. Be compassionate to yourself. Compassion is the ticket to higher consciousness. Remember that your cells are made up of this consciousness and they experience emotion.

2. Learn to build trust with the body and engage in the conversation so that you will have cooperation in overcoming and healing the ailment.

3. Allow changes in the conversation by using different thoughts and words that elicit spontaneous elevated emotions.

4. Your body is listening. When talking to it, realize that you are one with it, and you will most likely gain cooperation in healing the condition.

Therese had a chronic pain disorder. She spent an hour in meditation wondering if this would work. She states, "That night, after reaching a state of deep calm, I inwardly engaged my body in heartfelt conversation with hope but having no idea what to expect. After one hour, I began to notice something amazing happening. My tissues began to respond. Connective tissue pulled and stretched apart layers of scar tissue. Nerves fired and my calf muscles began to perform flexion and extension exercises independently of my conscious control. A calf muscle, that had become paralyzed by a neuropathic condition, came back to life as electric-like jolts shot through the area."

We are never victims to pain. We are givers and receivers of energy and our interpretation of it. Forgiveness, self-esteem, balance, and communication are always "get out of jail free" cards for becoming more aware of higher consciousness, adaption, acceptance of your own forthright decisions, and gratitude of yourself.

In the studies from the Institute of HeartMath, they have discovered that compassion and gratitude are the highest frequencies of the heart to promote connection and freedom to your life. Your heart rhythms can be used *for* you, and that is better than the other way around. The heart uses you when you are not aware.

For example, let's say that you have had a rough relationship. It made you cry several times. Finally, the partner leaves you, and you think: that's the last of that! However, the heart doesn't heal unless we put closure to this, mostly from our own desire to have a better life, and take that responsibility by either recognizing that we are a beautiful soul, or/and by forgiving ourselves for not getting out of that situation sooner. If we don't experience that closure, the pattern continues and we get driven down. Sooner or later, we may finally have had enough and finally put our foot down, but the sooner the better, right? My old mentor used to say, "You can learn the easy way or the hard way." Learning the hard way takes so much longer and can be a grueling process!

Now, if you fall in love, the heart rhythm changes. You use your heart for the better when you apply the intention. Saying to yourself, "Somebody loves me" creates the heart rate to speed up and because that statement is receiving a high vibration, your blood flow becomes healthy and you feel good. Can that change a pattern? It certainly can, as long as you remember that you are choosing your emotional wellbeing.

When it comes to self-esteem, it's a matter of being aware (in tune) with your passions. That has to come first. When we decide to lose a pattern intentionally, we must make other plans or goals to accomplish changing the same old behavior. Now is the time to really do that, since our spirit is becoming more profoundly in alignment to our higher self.

The astrological connection we have at birth teaches us we have a blueprint. How we *use* that blueprint is free will. I was recently given information from spirit that we are watching the world collapse, but not to be afraid of it. It is intentional, so we can rebuild ourselves *and* the world. When we change ourselves, we are contributing to changing the world. In a few years, we will see the results in a way that we are creating today.

Community, teamwork, sustainable living, spiritual and organic shifts within and without, are the new (yet ancient) connection we have been waking up to become. When we understand that we don't know everything, it leaves us humble and wide open to see that we are all one source with different ideas coming together to re-create what we learned when we were on the other side.

Talking to the self is actually that little voice inside that gets stronger in the silence. We simply can't ignore the daily expansion, and this is why people are feeling that they know there's more, but where is it?? Where do we look?

Who do we follow? What book do we read? The list goes on, so this is where I suggest you just get quiet, go in to the heart, and know that you were born with the right to *already know* - but not from outside sources. You may resonate with the others on all these resources, but the real Source is within you!

We have biorhythms that come together, and then grow apart, then come together again. These are daily cycles recorded from cyclical patterns of your physical, emotional, and mental activities. This theory was developed by Wilhelm Fliess in the late nineteenth century. The United States made it popular in the seventies, however some scientists think that these are nothing more than "chance." In my opinion, not only are these real, they are the measurement of our cycles. There are even apps available on your smartphone to view these. Normally, you can feel the way a day will go. It's a matter of paying attention and honoring it by "going with the flow."

CONCEPTS OF LIFE ITSELF

Life is not necessarily hard. "Hard" is a perspective that makes us feel that things are not going the way we suspect they should be. Thinking like this insists that we have to put effort into everything we do to hopefully get what we want. But this is an uphill climb. Life is big, and it certainly can be challenging. When we say to ourselves that life is hard, we have just confirmed we will live a hard life, and the more we are emotionally attached to that idea, the more we will have to live it.

Sound has a vibration which speaks a thousand words, and when attached to the intent, will confirm and direct energy to respond. That's why the magnitude of your words matter. Your convictions matter. Your emotions in your words matter. Emotions like hate never really go away, unless you are conscious of it and change it. In many cases, this is why we relive patterns based on words we have spoken in the past with conviction. The interesting point about the energetic field is that it will recreate a pattern that will then repeat a lesson you never finished.

Here is an example: "How come I keep picking the same guy over and over? Can't I find a partner that loves me?" Or, "No matter how many times I tell her I love her, she won't believe me."

So many times, I think of quotes from the bible, like the few I've mentioned previously in this book. I tend to use these a lot when I am speaking in groups. Downloads happen differently for everyone, and how people interpret things is individual. I also like, "In the beginning was the Word, and the Word was made flesh." (John 1:1)

This to me means that we are all created equal with the love and balance through our atoms, cells, tissue, DNA, etc. There is no stone left unturned when creation is at work. I'm certainly not a bible scholar and have no intention to become one, however to me, this is obvious. And what's even more clear is that we have divine energy working within the body.

Nothing is concrete. Bone is alive. All parts, including tissue, are moveable. Microscopes that see into the body at lightning speeds do not detect only the physical form. They see beyond the dense physical into the electrons, which get amazing results with much higher resolution. New technology has a way of seeing that we are created with the actual space between the cells, not just the cells. Can you actually view your body as a being in a vast and complex entanglement of light and sound? You can with your imagination, and you'll probably be right!

When it comes to meditation, we can create as we feel. Therefore, sending love and light to an area of the body and seeing an ailment as a temporary glitch due to stuck emotions, we can release them through meditation. We are capable of anything we put our minds to.

We can also override certain medication. One day I had a 12-year-old boy come into my office who had been adopted. His birth mother was a severe drug user, including heroin. He was known as a "crack baby" who was destined to go through withdrawals. I wasn't there and didn't see him as a child, but his adopted mother told me that he was an amazing young man. When I worked on him, I discovered this to be true!

He was still on Ritalin, a drug used to treat Attention-Deficit/Hyperactivity Disorder (ADHD) that targets Dopamine in the brain to reduce symptoms. Most people on Ritalin can go into a type of "numbing the senses" reaction, but not this young man. As I was doing a massage on him, I asked him what he'd like to be when he was older. His answer was that he'd like to be a doctor to help people not have to experience what he had to. He said that he has looked into it and thinks he could be a really good doctor. Of course, I applauded him and said I thought that was a wonderful idea! What was interesting was when I was telling him that, his eyes got big and his energy just kicked up with excitement. I said, "What kind of doctor appeals to you?" He said he'd like to be a neurologist or a psychologist.

The point is as he was talking to me, his energy shifted, and I felt him *rising above* the reaction of his medication. I will never forget that. A 12-year-old boy had impressed me to pieces, even though he was known as a "crack baby." (Yeah, cracking the code of using medicine and outsmarting it by rising above the side effects!)

We are all going through transitions. We simply cannot live like we used to with any kind of profound changes. We will have a new world of "shifts in perspectives" that are all about unity. It may take more challenges on our planet to get there, but it will one day happen.

I have worked to help people my whole life. I worked a lot and realized one day that I had to give myself a day off. Because I lived alone with my gorgeous dogs, I felt as though my energy was always able to be there for everyone. In the world we live in today, the old patterns we have lived are catching up with us as to remind us that this is not the way of our future. How can we possibly keep up with the pace, the expectations, the concepts of living only for others and still be healthy? We do that by learning, listening, and laughing! We must remember to breath and keep our sense of humor. That alone adds a few more years (and joy) to our lives.

CHAPTER EIGHT

~ LIVING HEAVEN ON EARTH ~

"We're entering a new world in which data may be more important than software." - Tim O'Reilly

Many philosophers have quoted their truthful concepts throughout time to help the world gain more knowledge. One of these books came out in the sixties, called *Positive Thinkers*. I know many people believe that our world today is too confused, chaotic and possibly turning catastrophic with the changes we are experiencing. However, the energies that each and every one of us contribute to the world is like a global goldmine!

We have the potential to eliminate forms of negativity occurring around us just by our conscious thoughts. It's a matter of understanding the reality of allowance. Surrender is the ticket for absolute open-minded consciousness to seep its way into our minds. The three-dimensional world we have lived in for thousands of years is collapsing right before our eyes, and this is the most important time in history. It is equivalent to our bodies in this scenario.

When we get sick, we need to find out how to heal. We search, we try things such as herbs, over the counter medicine or even vitamins to feel better. Then we discover it was the immune system that need a boost, or even what to do for allergies, the common cold, or any other ailment whether it be acute or chronic. We continue to search for a cure that works best for us. This teaches us that the more we learn, the more we can attribute to our own personal health. The world around us is very similar. Once we recognize that we are capable, powerful, aware, and amazing individuals, we will see that the statement, "As within, so without" is a true one. What better way to begin our connection to our higher self than to trust our own inner wisdom?

Recently I was doing a reading on a beautiful young lady who had recently become a Naturopathic doctor. Her spirit and her heart were angelic, like a soft fabric that you could feel comfort with over and over again. However, she was riddled with fear around people. She couldn't even go to the store without starting into a panic. Her patients were good, kind, and committed to her as they too could feel her love and compassion as a doctor. Because of her fear though, she called me for a session, and we went through her heart energy to *hear* what the energy of the cause was telling us.

I began to read where her father was overwhelmingly strong, to the point of having severe expectations on her. As the oldest child, she felt compelled to live up to that, however in her heart, natural medicine was the way to go. I sensed a strong soul and a beautiful, gentle heart that became confused by her upbringing, yet she remained truthful to herself.

Unfortunately, that did not come without its quirks. After a while of being around people, she would feel imperfect. Her subconscious was telling her that she would never be "up to par" and she began to retreat internally. When we were talking about it, she became shallow in her breathing and fear set in. I began to run energy in her to help calm her nerves in order to continue working. She was ready, and she was willing. Once we contacted the cause, she could breathe again. Her body allowed the energy to counteract her condition, giving her a sense of peace. Now she was able to identify this, and because she understood it, she refused to allow this to run her life any longer.

In one hour, we shifted her whole life from panic to peace.

I share these stories because they teach us how the many ways in which we were raised are coming to the surface, like the cream on top of the milk in the milk bottle. People think they are sick and need help for falling apart. It can look and feel grim for many as these inner discoveries are happening, however we must remember that with every dark cloud, the sun still shines. This is where we are today. A world of hurt is really a world of change. No longer do we have to depend on someone to always be there, because we are the ones who are always there!

How is it possible that we can create a new future for ourselves if we don't know how to do that? After working with many clients recently, I have received the following information: "Passion is in charge of how we move forward. The way to a better expanded future is to understand our passion. We are energy beings, therefore we live decisions every day. Are we ever really the same person when we wake up in the morning? This is not about judgement, but it is about what makes you get excited. What floats *your* boat?"

One of my clients loves photography, and it overrides all the pain she has carried. If she sees nature or a moment where she can take a cool picture, this makes her heart sing. We don't have to save the world or feel bad that we don't know how. I call this "saving yourself first." Even the body heals through passion. Remembering a beautiful moment of togetherness or laughter with a loved one lifts the spirit to be brighter. Passion is the key to happiness, and we can change our jobs, our hobbies, our input with confidence when we have passion. The cells take on a new production as the heart listens, aligns, and corrects a pattern. There is nothing stopping you.

A few weeks ago, I was curious about what the housing market was like in my area. I wasn't looking to move, I just looked for fun. What I saw were many houses on the market for outrageous costs. It was only information so I wasn't taking it personally or feeling that I couldn't afford a home, etc. However, I scrolled down the list and saw a house that caught my eye. It was perfect. There was a home, actually well-priced, that was drawing me with its perfection of beauty, tall ceilings, nice manicured lawn, etc. I looked further at the ad and noticed my heart began to get stronger in the beat (not faster). I noticed I was breathing with more excitement, almost as if I'd won the lottery! Even though I didn't need a new house, I truly feel this was a "meant to be" example so I could witness my reaction to what I considered the perfect home.

This can happen to all of us. Feeling with love is how the body ignites, wakes up, and creates. Was this passion in motion? Sure it was, and did it feed my heart to know down the road I will find another one when the time is right? Yes, because the energy is engaged now in my heart as a birthing. This is how we attract and manifest. It is all through passion, connection and allowance.

I decided to write on the topic of "heaven on Earth" because we are experiencing a dynamic in a world that is being exposed. Whether we like it or not, our juices can get flowing with the momentum of emotions. As this third-dimensional world falls apart, we can step in.

Shaman do not deny what is happening, as a matter of fact, they sense things way before they come to fruition. In the Cherokee tribe, they ask everyone the question: "The world was created for you. What will you do with it?" Trust is a factor that must be considered. It takes a lot of allowance to believe that you can trust someone, something, a decision, a changing of an experience, or even a statement. It's when we don't trust ourselves that we begin to distrust others.

YOUR ORIGINAL PLAN OF ACTION

As we look deep within our hearts, or into the peace within the soul, we can usually see how we can organize our desires by how our beliefs kick in and become real. In other words, without seeing a manifestation, we may never believe that there is any source of energy support. We may feel that life is unfair and isn't worth living. The truth is we didn't understand what path we were choosing. Beating our heads against the wall doesn't help, it just keeps hurting.

I have read enough people's energy and experienced my own understanding of manifestation that I realize we must have a plan A, B, and C in our soul:

PLAN A: All the lessons you encounter can be learned with an open mind and be created without fear. We were born to live lessons and make our own decisions to be stronger and wiser in our years for true happiness.

PLAN B: Try not to judge yourself by being mindful of lessons learned. Live life based on love and passion as much as possible, just from those lessons. Surrender to the past, see the beauty in all things, learn from living in the moment, and stop allowing others to run your life.

PLAN C: Give up and feel no one loves you, life is too hard, what's the point, etc. Not wanting to be here, longing for another world.

None of these plans are based on judgement. They are based on the heart and soul's desire. They are also there from lifetimes that lead us to this moment. People are bored with the past, which is why we have revolutions through evolutions.

The times we live in can make people feel that there is no use in living since everything is changing. In reality, we are making everything up all the time, so what is in us to be disappointed with world changes? Accepting life as an observer will help us to not feel squashed or alone. We simply have to see that humanity is trying to find its way. Yet a world that really never understood or accepted freedom of choice is where we must focus.

In the spiritual law, we learn that you don't mess with free will. It is every person's birthright to live according to their world, their lessons, their choices. Families have yet to really learn that lesson. So, we judge each other and think because someone doesn't agree with us that they must be wrong.

Unconditional love is the way of the future. It doesn't need a reason, a category, or even an opinion. It means we accept each other no matter what. Of course, we don't have to agree with each other, but acceptance is the key. It lightens your load, stops judgement from situations that *you* only knew, and better yet, helps with your expansion in your soul. THIS is what is meant to live heaven on earth. It even helps you realize that every person has a life, a lesson, and we are not to interfere... no matter who we are.

In reality, we are much deeper in connection than we have allowed. Life is an adventure. It's getting into that depth within that keeps us balanced, stable, less subconsciously guilty for not doing something that we thought we should have, etc. If it is true that everything we choose in life is about action, reaction, and non-action, (which it is) then we must begin to pursue a deeper connection and conscious agreement to how we initially respond to the now vs. then. What are we willing to accept, align to, agree to, or even become?

CELESTIAL MUSIC THROUGH TONING

"Our biological rhythms are the symphony of the cosmos, music embedded deep within us to which we dance, even when we can't name the tune" - Deepak Chopra

Your state of mind is the way in which we move forward in this world, and dreams and desires can come true! There are several ways in which we can manifest these and work on our own health.

One way that I love to do this is by toning my voice to intention. I previously had mentioned that music calms the body in stressful situations. I will share with you that intentional toning is a way that can also bring you back to a better state of mind, and possibly help with pain as well as regenerative strength throughout your body.

Here is a technique that I've used and really like:

Sit quietly without interruption and take three deep breaths. As you center yourself, let go of all that has happened during the day. When you feel ready, from your gut, take a big breath and then hum a tone for the exhale. Do this a few times until you resonate and feel a little bit like you are buzzing. The hum is a biofeedback within the body that resonates to the cells. Now apply an intention. You might have a need, or a desire to release subconscious patterns. Even that alone will connect you to the subconscious. Remember that energy and intention are how the process works, and it is allowance that will manifest it into the field, which then affects the heart. Taking a breath in changes the direction of thought when we release the breath.

It doesn't matter what tone you use, as long as you can feel it resonate with the intention. I have seen where people's pain diminishes extremely quickly. Anywhere from headaches to knee pain will dissipate with consistency with your intent on a daily basis.

Sound is an awesome inspiration and healer, whether you are listening to the music you love, or singing your favorite song. Memories tend to stay in the body when you hear good music. A song you heard as a child will bring back all the feelings when it comes on the radio, and it might even be of a loved one who crossed over. Maybe that loved one is wanting to connect with you, and you may have chills when the song is played.

For me, when I hear a song that reminds me of a loved one, I feel peace and the joy that person brought to my life. Nicola Tesla's quote I mentioned earlier once again rings true when he said, "If you want to find the secrets of the universe, you must think in terms of energy, frequency, and vibration." Because we are pure spirit in physical bodies, we can associate this quote to be true when we direct our minds to this wisdom. Sound is frequency and vibration, and you are using your intention as directing the energy.

Cymatics is a scientific term meaning the study of sound, or "wave phenomena." It can also be said that it is an actual therapy in which sound waves are directed at the body with the aim of promoting health. The definition from *Wiktionary* says "Cymatics is the study of visible sound and vibration. Typically, a surface of a plate, diaphragm, or membrane is vibrated, and regions of maximum and minimum displacement are made visible in a thin coating of particles, paste or liquid. Different patterns emerge in the medium depending on the geometry of the plate and the driving frequency."

So basically, it means that a pattern emerges when tone is applied. Whether it be in a dish with sand or toward the body, we connect the tone. If done with a plate on top of a speaker with one specific tone running through it, you will see a visible pattern. Change the tone, change the pattern. This affects the whole body, just like a plate of sand on the speaker.

We are the universe in a nutshell. Sometimes I feel the answers are so clear for us to comprehend, however our insecurities are the culprit for feeling trapped. In the world today, we are heading for this wake-up to be presented on any level that seems adequate. Our government, our atmosphere, climate change, etc. The most important point of this book is to remind us all that we are not victims to or of anything. Egos are just another form of insecurity trying to look important. Truly, spirit doesn't need that at all. Why do we?

The old concepts of protection are what draw to us that which we feel we need protection from. Being in *new times* means that we are surrendering ourselves to the trust of our own soul. Our hearts are begging to be heard as to live in homeostasis and balance. Giving to yourself is just as important as giving to anything. Receiving is even more important so that we have enough energy to continue giving. Living your life from the inside out is about creating yourself, identifying what and who you truly are, and actually loving yourself.

Many years ago, my Cherokee mentor had mentioned to me in passing that "the only thing that spirit asks of us is to love ourselves. It is the easiest thing to do and the hardest thing to do." Learning that has taken a while, however I never forgot it. I strived for it and now live it. I feel now is the time to share that with you.

Starting over only means we begin to recognize that we really do live in the moment, and that's it. It's leaving the past behind that is difficult. Yet, by doing that, you also find that forgetting and forgiving becomes automatic. You are a shining and brilliant star. In the world of celestial movement through open-minded change, we can have a divine life. It's up to us on how fast we learn lessons. Emotionally, mentally and spiritually, we are creating the world we desire, inside and out.

My deepest wish and dream for humanity is to find unconditional love for ourselves, creating new beginnings in a unified world, and appreciation for our Earth. Here's to you my friends, and the reality of truth!

CONCLUSION

If you take anything away from this book, please let it be that you are in charge of your life. At the end of this adventure we call our life, we will have to have a *life review* on the other side. It would be so ideal to know that you lived in the moment, became conscious of your choices, and found life to offer you everything that was possible. We have lived someone else's ideas for far too long.

Speaking from experience, the meaning of illness is holding onto something that no longer suits us. The bottom line is that any illness is preventable, not just with the food you eat, proper exercise, etc., but the way in which you perceive life. If this doesn't come first, no matter what you do, no matter how many pills or vitamins you take, you will never achieve the peace of mind you **so** deserve, and that is your ultimate destiny.

Our human race needs each and every one of us to acknowledge what truly matters, which is universal love. Gone are the days of the matrix leading our world into disaster. Releasing false expectations of ourselves or others will be known as the awakening of a lifetime. What we choose to hold onto or release is the choice we all face. Life is emerging into a telepathic awareness of all things. In the movie "Jurassic Park", Jeff Goldblum's character says, "Life always finds a way." I have seen, witnessed, and contributed in many amazing quantum healings that are deeply profound. Therefore, I have learned - and know - that *no-thing* is ever impossible.

ABOUT THE AUTHOR

Mona Delfino is an author and world-renowned Energy Medicine Practitioner of 40 years. She was born a shaman, learning her calling and helping people and animals heal from a very early age. Mona is well-versed in spirituality and Quantum Healing, teaching the Art of Alchemy: as within, so without. She has an extensive background of reading her clients from afar as well as seeing them in person; Energy has no bounds. Her effective and deliberate work has helped heal thousands over the years, as well as working for the Earth. When feeling called, she responds and does ceremony to release memory from gridlines throughout the world for energetic cleansing.

Mona is able to put an understanding to the "big picture" through reading the energy of humanity through astrological patterns as well as inside each individual. She continually teaches the sacred language of the human body. She even wrote the book on it!

Mona offers individual healing sessions that are done over Skype, phone, and sometimes in person. She also holds spiritual retreats that are timely and relevant for all who attend. Current topics include the "Spiritual Immune System", the "Energetic Membrane" and the "Sacred Language of the Human Body".

Made in the USA
San Bernardino, CA
31 October 2019